Larry Richard

THREDPGILL

SCIENCE FUN WITH MILK CARTONS

WHITTLESEY HOUSE
McGRAW-HILL BOOK COMPANY, INC.
NEW YORK   TORONTO   LONDON

HERMAN SCHNEIDER IS SCIENCE CONSULTANT
FOR THE ELEMENTARY SCHOOLS OF NEW YORK CITY

SCIENCE
FUN *with*
MILK CARTONS

by HERMAN *and* NINA SCHNEIDER

pictures by JEANNE BENDICK

SCIENCE FUN WITH MILK CARTONS

Library of Congress Catalog Card Number: 52-13466

SECOND PRINTING

Published by Whittlesey House
A division of the McGraw-Hill Book Company, Inc.
PRINTED IN THE UNITED STATES OF AMERICA

To our good neighbors, with thanks
for all the empty milk cartons

CONTENTS

SCIENCE FUN WITH MILK CARTONS

MOVING DAY IS HERE

EVERY DAY is moving day for you. Every day you move things—your bicycle, your books, your skates, yourself, and packages and bundles of all kinds. You move on foot and on wheels, by muscle power and by engine power. You work at transportation many times each day.

Many people make a living at transportation. Bus drivers, pilots, locomotive engineers, taxi drivers, elevator operators—these are just a few of the transportation jobs that people work at.

Because transportation is such an important part of the world's work, people have invented many ways of making the work easier. They have invented ways of moving things on wheels and in boats, over bridges and through canals, with the power of wind, water, gasoline, steam, and electricity to help with the transportation.

In this book you will find out about some of the machines that people have invented to make the moving work easier. You will also find out how to build simple working models of these inventions.

Through reading and building, you will find out many things about the science of transportation.

BUILDING MODELS WITH MILK CARTONS

ALL THE MODELS described in this book can be built with milk cartons. Square-ended quart cartons were used, but you can build many of the models with peaked-top cartons and with other sizes just as well.

You will find that milk cartons are excellent for model building. They cost you nothing, they are easy to cut and bend, and they are strong and waterproof. You can paint them with oil colors, bronze paint, or aluminum paint. Best of all, after you build a model you can keep it. You don't have to take it apart to build another model. You just get more empty milk cartons.

Besides the milk cartons, you will need some other supplies and tools. Here they are:

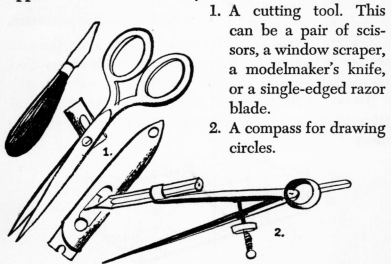

1. A cutting tool. This can be a pair of scissors, a window scraper, a modelmaker's knife, or a single-edged razor blade.

2. A compass for drawing circles.

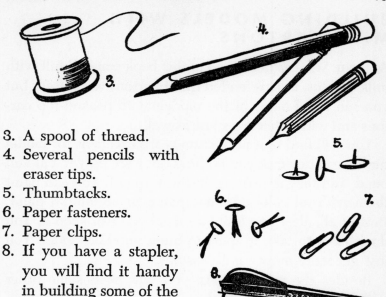

3. A spool of thread.
4. Several pencils with eraser tips.
5. Thumbtacks.
6. Paper fasteners.
7. Paper clips.
8. If you have a stapler, you will find it handy in building some of the models, but it is not absolutely necessary.

One important thing to remember is to rinse the milk cartons in cold water as soon as they have been emptied, because the remaining milk will turn sour quickly.

To keep your tools and supplies from wandering off, store them in a milk container with one long side cut away.

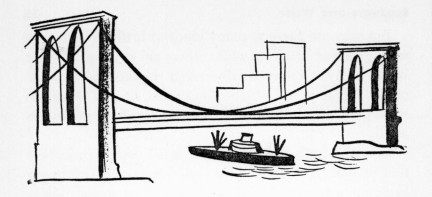

ROADWAYS OVER WATER

YOU HAVE SEEN many kinds of bridges, of many shapes and sizes, made of all kinds of materials. But all bridges are alike in one important way. They are all roadways. They all carry traffic—people or cars or trains or animals. And they carry this traffic over some kind of drop or hollow or body of water. A 5-foot wooden plank across a brooklet is a bridge, and so is the 5-mile-long steel and concrete San Francisco-Oakland Bay Bridge. Both are roadways over water.

But why are there so many kinds of bridges? Why are some made of concrete while others are made of steel or wood? Why are some made so that they can turn, while others lift, and still others don't move at all? Why are some built with huge towers, while others have no towers at all?

Every bridge is built the way it is because it works best that way in that place. There are reasons for building a bridge in a certain shape, or of a certain material. These are reasons you can understand, and after you have built the simple bridge models described in this book, you will understand them even better.

DRAWBRIDGES

You have probably seen drawbridges in pictures of old castles. Such drawbridges were built for protection. When a nobleman planned to build a castle he tried to locate it in the safest possible place. The top of a hill was a good place. An island was fine. In either case he could see any enemies before they came close enough to spring a surprise attack. If no island was handy, the nobleman built an island. He had a deep ditch dug all around the castle, and then flooded the ditch with water. This flooded ditch was called a moat. The moat kept out unwelcome visitors, but it also kept in the nobleman and his people. To permit them to enter or leave the island castle, a drawbridge was built.

A drawbridge is a movable bridge. It can be let down to join the castle to the surrounding land, and it can be raised to remove the roadway in time of danger. A drawbridge can make a castle into an island fortress.

You can make a working model of a drawbridge. You will need 2 milk cartons (rinsed out with cold water), a pencil, a hairpin (or paper clip), some thread, and a knife or scissors.

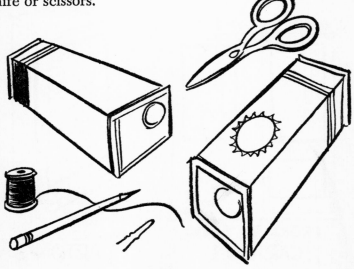

This is how your model drawbridge will look when it is finished.

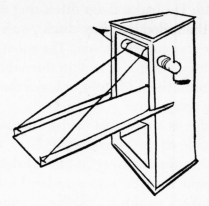

'1. With a sharp pencil, draw the lines shown on the pictures of each carton.

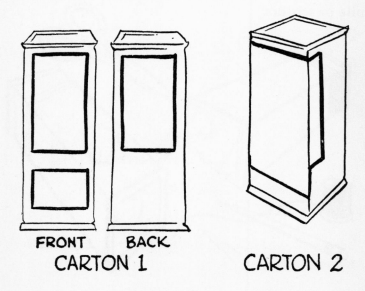

FRONT   BACK

CARTON 1   CARTON 2

2. Now cut along the lines. When you are finished you will have 2 pieces that look like this. One piece will be the castle tower, and the other will be the drawbridge that is raised and lowered by the sentries.

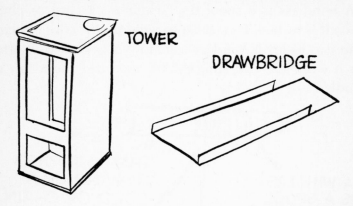

TOWER

DRAWBRIDGE

3. Now cut a slit like this in each side of the drawbridge piece.

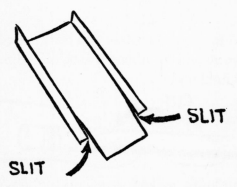

SLIT

SLIT

This will allow the drawbridge to fit into the castle tower.

But we're not ready to put the two pieces together yet. First we have to build the machinery that raises and lowers the drawbridge. This machinery is called a windlass, and it makes the raising and lowering job easier.

A windlass is a spool that winds up a cord or chain when it is turned. It is easier to wind up the cord or chain than it is to lift it hand over hand. (A bucket well often has a windlass, and ship chains, too, are wound up on windlasses.)

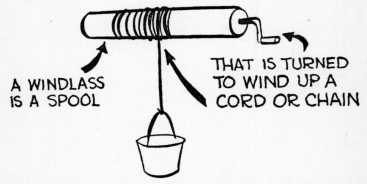

A WINDLASS IS A SPOOL

THAT IS TURNED TO WIND UP A CORD OR CHAIN

The spool for your windlass will be a pencil. The cord you wind on it will be about 2 feet of ordinary thread, any color you choose.

CUT

1. With your knife, make 2 little cuts in the pencil. These cuts will allow you to fasten the 2 ends of the thread to the pencil without having to tie knots.

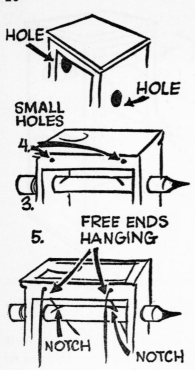

HOLE

HOLE

SMALL
HOLES

4.

3.

FREE ENDS
5.   HANGING

NOTCH   NOTCH

2. Next, bore 2 holes in the castle tower. An easy way to do this is with the point of your scissors or with a sharp-pointed pencil. Make the holes just large enough for your pencil to fit in snugly.
3. Push the pencil through the 2 holes.
4. Then make 2 small holes at the top of the tower.
5. Now pass one end of the thread through one of the holes and fasten it to the pencil by slipping it into one of the notches.
6. Do the same with the other end of the thread.

Now you are ready to assemble the drawbridge and tower.

1. First make 2 small cuts at the far end of the bridge (the end without the slits), to hold the thread in place.
2. Then slip the bridge into place against the tower.
3. Pass the thread into the 2 small cuts, and you're all set.

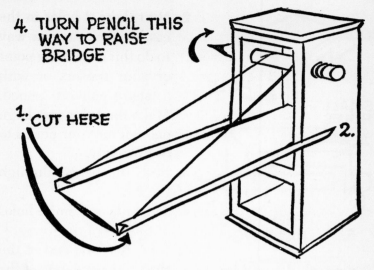

4. TURN PENCIL THIS
   WAY TO RAISE
   BRIDGE

1. CUT HERE

2.

4. Turn the pencil one way and the bridge goes up; turn
   it the other way and the bridge drops down into place,
   ready for traffic.

   Perhaps you'd like to have a handle for turning your
windlass. You can make it easily out of a bent hairpin or
paper clip.

   To fasten the handle to the pencil, first push a pin, a
needle, or the point of a compass through the eraser tip.
Then push the handle through the hole you have made.
Now your windlass is complete.

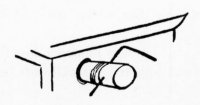

Your little drawbridge is easy to raise and lower, because it weighs very little and is barely strong enough to carry a squad of marching mice. Real drawbridges are much heavier. They were built strong enough to carry knights in full armor, horses, carriages, and other such weighty things. To raise and lower a real drawbridge could be quite a job for one man, or even several men. But the job was made easy by two heavy pieces of stone or iron called counterweights.

Here is how you can at-
tach two little counter-
weights to your model drawbridge. Notice how they pull
down on the thread, helping
to raise the bridge.

In the same way, the counterweights on a castle draw-
bridge pulled down on the chains attached to the bridge, making it easier for the sentries to raise it.

In the olden days, drawbridges over moats were used for protection. Nowadays they are built over rivers, not for protection, but for carrying traffic across. They are raised to permit high-masted ships to sail through.

Most modern drawbridges are raised and lowered by machinery, so that the bridge attendant's job is not very difficult. He merely presses the switch that starts the machinery going.

It costs money to run a drawbridge. The attendant must be paid, the machinery must be kept in order, and electricity is needed to run it. Wouldn't it be cheaper to build an ordinary bridge, high enough to permit boats to sail under it? It would, if automobiles could climb ladders. But since they can't, it is necessary to build long sloping roadways to help the automobiles to climb up the bridge, and to climb down the other side. These roadways are expensive too, so sometimes it's cheaper to build a drawbridge.

However, there are other things to think about. When a drawbridge is raised, it stops being a bridge and turns into a traffic block for the roadway. This can become quite a nuisance on a busy river, with lots of high-masted boats calling for attention. On such a river a high bridge, with its expensive long roadways, is better than a drawbridge with no roadways at all.

But where the river traffic is not too busy, a drawbridge is fine.

BASCULE BRIDGES

A bascule (băs'-kūl) bridge does the same kind of job as a drawbridge. It is a movable bridge. In its "up" position, it allows river traffic to move, while in its "down" position it becomes a roadway for automobiles and other dry-land traffic. Bascule bridges are usually cheaper and simpler to build than drawbridges, because they have no towers. It takes time and money to build towers.

A bascule bridge can do without a tower because the machinery is underneath the bridge. This machinery is usually operated by a powerful electric motor, but your homemade model will be a one-mousepower job, operated by a windlass.

Now let's get started with the building of your bascule bridge. You will need 2 milk cartons (don't forget about rinsing them with cold water), 2 feet of thread, a pencil, a hairpin or paper clip, a compass, and a dozen pins. A stapler will be handy, but not absolutely necessary.

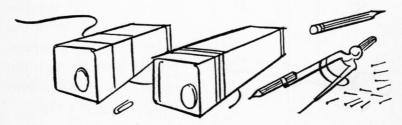

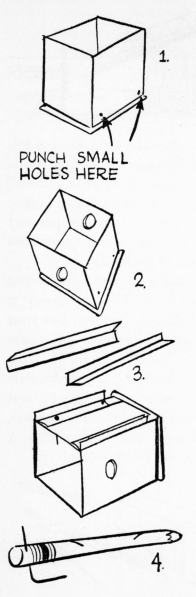

PUNCH SMALL
HOLES HERE

The first part to build is the pier, the part that holds the roadway and that contains the machinery.

1. Cut one of the cartons in half, and then punch 2 small holes with the point of your compass.

2. With the sharp point of a pencil, make 2 larger holes, 1 at each side. These should be just large enough to permit a tight fit of your pencil.

3. From the remaining half of the carton, cut 2 strips out of the corner. These strips will be the tracks to guide your bascule bridge as it rolls back and forth over the pier. With pins or staples, fasten them to the top of the pier.

4. Now prepare the windlass. Cut 2 small notches in your pencil. With the point of your compass, push a hole through the eraser, and push in a bent hairpin or paper clip.

Now you're ready to build the main part of the bridge
—the part called the span. There are two ways to build
this. The first way is very easy and will take about 15
minutes. The second way is harder and takes longer, but
the bridge will look much more like a real one. The best
idea is to build your bridge the first way, assemble it,
have fun with it for a while, and then put in the
finishing touches that will change your bridge into the
more real-looking type.

1. Spread the points of your compass until they are as
   wide apart as the width of a milk carton. Then draw a
   curve on the other carton, as the picture shows.

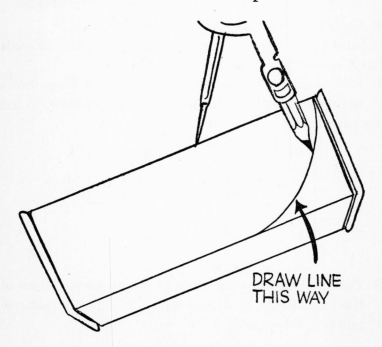

DRAW LINE
THIS WAY

2. Do the same on the other side of the carton.

3. With your knife or scissors, cut along the curved lines you have drawn and straight across the carton. With the compass point, punch a hole in each side. Now your carton looks like this.

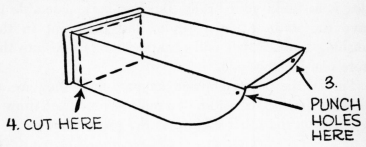

4. CUT HERE

3.
PUNCH
HOLES
HERE

4. Cut away the other side of the carton.

Now you're ready to assemble the two parts of your bascule bridge—the pier and the span.

1. Push the pencil-windlass through the 2 large holes in the pier. Stick the hairpin or paper clip through the eraser.

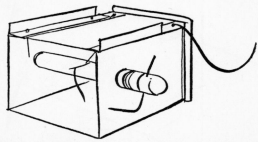

2. Push one end of your piece of thread through one of the holes in the pier, and then slip it firmly into one notch in the pencil.

3. Now guide the other end of the thread through the 2 holes in the span, then down through the other hole in the pier, and into the other notch in the pencil-windlass.

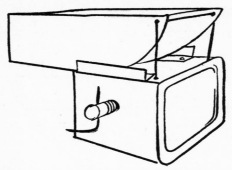

Now you're all set to operate your bascule bridge. Turn the handle of the windlass until most of the thread has been wound up on the pencil. Then, as you turn the handle still further, you will see the span rise. Turn the handle the other way and the span will slowly move down into place, just like a real bascule bridge.

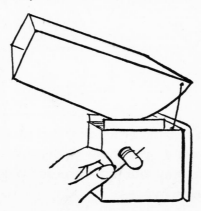

After you've operated this simple type of bridge for a while, you'll probably want to add improvements that make your bridge look more like the real thing. Here's how.

1. Unwind the thread and remove the span.
2. Cut 3-cornered pieces out of the sides of the span, as shown.

3.
TOP

2.
SIDES

3. Cut 3-cornered pieces out of the top of the span.
4. Reassemble the pier and the span, and you're all set.

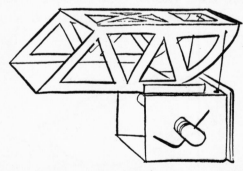

Perhaps you're wondering why 3-cornered pieces are cut out. Why not 4 or 5 corners? Because a real bridge is also built that way, out of 3-cornered pieces called triangles. Let's see why.

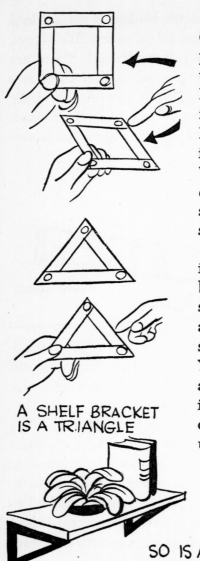

Make a 4-cornered form out of cardboard strips and paper fasteners. Hold it like this.

If you push it at any place, it collapses like this.

Now make a 3-cornered form, a triangle.

When you push it, it doesn't collapse. A triangle is stronger than a 4-cornered shape.

The triangle shape is used in many other things besides bascule bridges. An ordinary shelf bracket is a triangle, and so is the bracket that supports a hanging sign. You'll find thousands of triangles in most steel bridges, in cranes and cars, in many of the common things you use every day.

A SHELF BRACKET
IS A TRIANGLE

SO IS A SIGN BRACKET

LUNCH

Now let's look at a real bascule bridge. It doesn't look quite like your Milk-carton Special, of course. It's bigger, and it's made of steel instead of cardboard. There are two other important differences. One is that there is a curious-looking thing sticking up at one end, and the other is that there are no ropes or cables like the threads in your little bridge. Let's find out more about these two differences.

COUNTERWEIGHT

The curious-looking thing at one end is a counterweight. It is very heavy, made of steel and concrete, and it does the same kind of work as the counterweight in a drawbridge. It makes the lifting job easier.

There are no cables or ropes on a real bascule bridge, because this type of bridge is not worked by a windlass turned by hand. Instead, the work is done by an electric motor. The motor turns a small wheel with teeth in it, called a gear. This gear turns a larger gear attached to the span, or roadway. In this way the motor turns and lifts the span, and when it turns in the opposite direction, it lowers the span back into place.

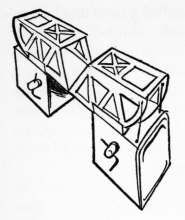

Sometimes a river is too wide for a bascule bridge, and yet some kind of movable bridge is needed. The answer is simple—two bascule bridges working end to end. Perhaps there is such a pair in your town. If not, here is a picture of two model bridges sharing the work between them.

SWING BRIDGES

Here is another kind of movable bridge, called a swing bridge. This kind swings around to make room for boats to pass through. When it swings sideways, boats can sail by on either side of it. When it swings back into place, cars and trucks can roll across.

A swing bridge is sometimes called a turntable bridge, because it turns on a kind of table. This table, made of steel and stone, supports the bridge and also contains the machinery that does the turning. Like any table, it needs to rest on some kind of floor. The floor of a turntable bridge may be an island in the middle of the river, if there happens to be such an island handy. Otherwise the bridgebuilders must rest the table on a solid floor, which is the bedrock underneath the river.

But how can the workmen work at the bottom of the river? Do they work in diving suits, or do they have machinery that works by remote control? Perhaps you have wondered about this before. You can find the answer by trying a simple little experiment.

You will need a drinking glass, a sheet of paper, and a basin of water. Cram the paper into the bottom of the glass. Hold the glass upside down and push it all the way down into the water. Does the water rise into the glass? You will see that it doesn't. Then, to make sure, lift out the glass and take out the paper. You will find that it is dry. The air in the glass kept the water from coming in.

AIR IN THE GLASS

KEEPS THE
WATER OUT

In the same way, workmen can work under water without getting wet. A huge steel tank, like a tremendous drinking glass, protects the workmen. This tank, called a caisson, is lowered into the water until it touches bottom. The bottom of the caisson is open, but no water can enter, because the air keeps it out and because an air pump forces more air into the caisson. The men come into the caisson through a special opening called an air lock. Then they climb down a ladder to reach the river bottom. There they can work under water without having to wear diving suits. They dig away the mud to get to bedrock. Then they pour in concrete and let it harden. On top of the concrete they build the "table" that supports the bridge and its machinery.

Now let's get on with our model bridge. You will need 2 milk cartons, a pencil, a paper fastener, a hairpin or paper clip, and a piece of twine about 1 foot long.

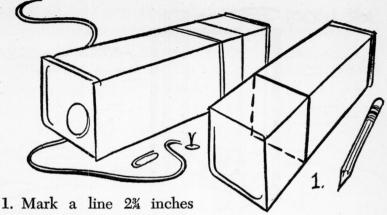

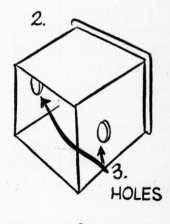

1. Mark a line 2¾ inches from the bottom of one carton, all the way around.

2. Cut all around on this line. The piece you cut away will be your pier— the part on which the span turns.

3. With a sharp-pointed pencil, make 2 holes in the pier. The windlass will go through these holes, so make them just large enough for a snug fit.

4. Make a small hole in the top of the pier, and 2 holes in the sides.

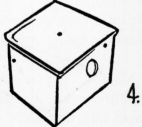

5. Now we're ready to build the span. Take the other
   carton and cut it as the picture shows. The cutting is
   quite simple, because all you need to do is cut out one
   triangle after the other. You know now why triangles
   are stronger than other shapes. (If not, you can find
   the answer on page 30.)

Now for the grand job of assembling the pier and span.

1. First make a handle out of a bent hairpin or paper
   clip, and push it into the eraser of your pencil.

2. Make a small hole in the middle of the roadway.

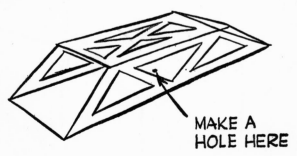

MAKE A
HOLE HERE

3. Place the span on the pier and push the paper fastener through both holes—the one in the roadway and the one in the top of the pier. Then bend apart the 2 ends of the paper fastener.

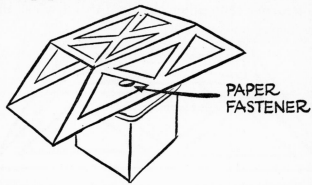

PAPER
FASTENER

Now for the machinery that turns the bridge. This machinery is quite simple, yet your friends will puzzle for hours without being able to figure it out. Here's the great secret.

1. Tie one end of the twine to the middle of the span.
2. Pass the other end of the twine through one of the holes in the top of the pier.

3. Push the pencil-and-handle piece into the 2 holes prepared for it.

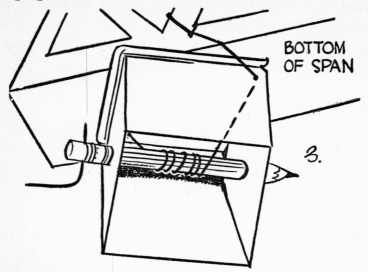

BOTTOM
OF SPAN

3.

4. Wind the twine 5 or 6 times around the pencil, and then pass the end up through the other hole in the top of the pier.

5. Pull the twine tight and tie it around the middle of the span, right next to the first knot you tied.

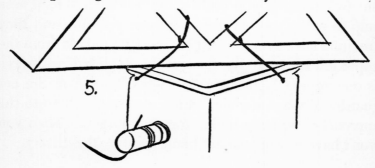

5.

Now you're all set. Turn the handle one way, and the span will rotate slowly to its open position—ready to allow river traffic to sail through. Turn it the other way, and the span will close—ready for bridge traffic to ride.

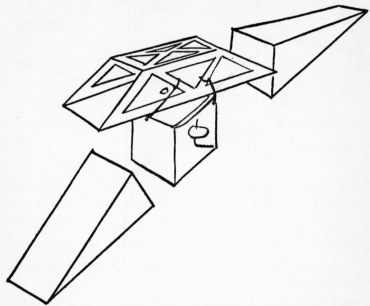

Here's a picture of the model bridge in action. Notice the two slanting approaches, one on each side. These help to make your bridge look more realistic, and they are quite easy to make. Just cut a carton in half, from the upper left corner to the lower right. Each half will serve as one approach. If you're extra-ambitious, you can cut guardrails out of another carton and staple them to the approaches, to keep traffic from tumbling off. Then you won't have to worry about being sued by the drivers.

Science Fun with Milk Cartons

LIFT BRIDGES

It's harder to stand on one foot than on two. You get tired much sooner. This is true of people, ducks, chimpanzees, ostriches—and bridges. Bridges don't get tired, of course, but they do something else—they bend. Look at a picture of a bascule bridge. When it is in the "up-and-downstream" position it is really standing on one foot, and it bends. To keep it from bending too far, the bridge is strengthened with all sorts of braces along its sides. A swing bridge, too, when it is open for river traffic, is standing on one foot. It, too, must be strengthened to keep it from bending too far.

Bridges are often strengthened with braces. These braces, which are called trusses, are made of steel and are quite heavy. A long bridge would need many more braces than a short bridge, of course. A very long bridge would need so many trusses that it would be very, very heavy to lift, and very expensive. For this reason, it is not practical to build a one-footed bridge—such as a bascule bridge or a swing bridge—over a very wide river.

Instead, another kind of bridge is built. This is called a lift bridge, and it is the kind that always stands on two feet.

The two feet of a lift bridge are its two towers. The span itself is supported by strong cables attached to the towers. The span can be lifted by machinery to allow boats to pass through, and then can be lowered again for dry-land traffic to travel across. Because it never has to stand on one foot, the span does not have to be strengthened with many enormous, heavy, and expensive trusses.

To build your model lift bridge, you will need 3 milk cartons, a pencil, 4 thumbtacks or paper fasteners, a paper clip or hairpin, and about 8 feet of thread. You will also need a base for supporting your bridge. This can be a strip of orange-crate wood or corrugated cardboard, about 2 feet long and 4 inches wide.

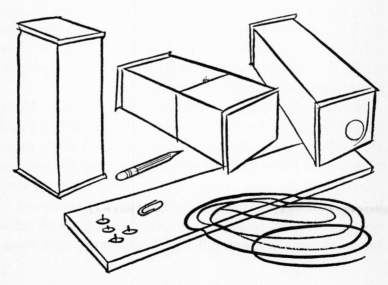

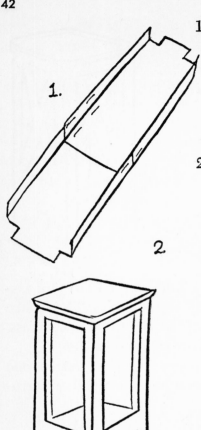

1.

2

1. To build the span, cut off 2 sides of a milk carton. Fasten them together to make 1 long strip. Cut 2 little corners off at each end, as shown, to leave a sort of "tongue."

2. Now for the towers. These can be plain or fancy. The plain ones will work fine, while the fancy ones will look much more real but will take about half an hour of extra work on your part. Here are front and side views of a plain tower, and here you have the fancy type.

**PLAIN
TOWER**

**FANCY
TOWER**

3. Punch 2 holes in one of the towers to allow a snug fit of the pencil-windlass that will raise and lower the span. (If you have forgotten how to make the windlass, look back at page 19.)

NOTCHES

3.

4.

4. Cut 2 notches in the pencil, to be used later for fastening the thread that will act as cables. Then make a hole in the eraser, using the point of the compass. Push a bent hairpin or paper clip into the hole.

5. With 2 thumbtacks or paper fasteners, fasten one tower to one end of the orange-crate wood or corrugated paper base.

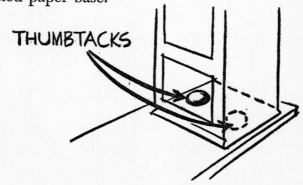

THUMBTACKS

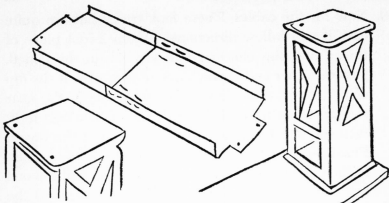

6. With the compass point, make 2 holes at the top of each tower and 2 holes at each end of the span.

7. Now put the span into place, with the "tongue" fitting into the space in the tower. Then fasten the other tower in place, using 2 thumbtacks. The span should have enough room to move up and down without scraping against the towers.

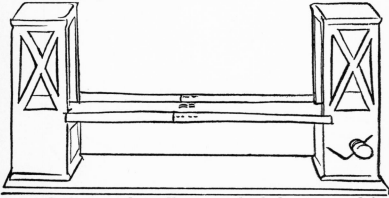

8. Push the pencil-windlass into the holes prepared for it in step 3.

9. Now for the cables. These look tricky but are quite easy if you follow directions. Take a 2-foot piece of thread and slip one end into a notch in the pencil. Pass the other end through one of the holes at the top of the tower, then down through a hole in the near side of the span, up through the other hole next to it, then through the other hole at the top of the tower. Finish off by slipping the thread into the second notch in the pencil. If you turn the pencil, you will see one side of the span lift up. Now you have to connect the other end of the span to make it lift. Step 10 will take care of this.

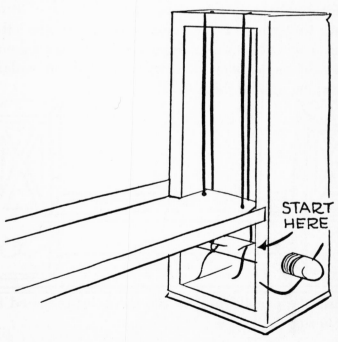

10. Do the same thing that you did in step 9, but this time use a 6-foot piece of thread, and pass it through the holes in both towers and the far end of the span. Perhaps this sounds complicated, so let's take it one step at a time:

    a. Take one end of the 6-foot thread and slip it into one notch in the pencil.

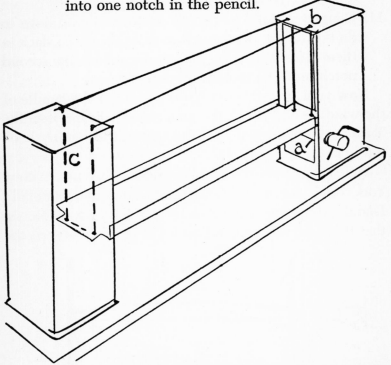

    b. Take the other end of the thread and pass it up through a hole in the tower (you'll find the other thread in that hole, too, but it won't get in the way).

    c. Then pass the end of the thread through a hole in the other tower, then down through a hole in the far end of the span, then up through the other hole in the span, up through the other hole in that tower, back through the other hole in the tower with the pencil in it, and finally into the second notch in the pencil.

11. Congratulations, you made it! Now all you have to do is even out the threads so that there is no slack in them. This is done by pulling the ends in the second notch until the threads are straight.

Now your bridge is ready for use. Turn the handle of the windlass and watch the span rise slowly and steadily. Turn it the other way and the span settles gently back into place.

Here's a picture of a real lift bridge. This one, in New York City, connects Manhattan Island and Randall's Island, which are separated by the East River. Notice that there are no overhead cables to be seen, such as the

ones in your model bridge. The reason why there are no such cables is that the real bridge has two machines, one in each tower. Each machine raises its own end of the span. As you can guess, the two machines must be carefully regulated so that they run at exactly the same speed. Otherwise, one end of the span would move faster than the other, and the span would be tipped into a crooked position.

If you want your model bridge to look more like the real kind, without overhead cables, you can make the change very easily. Just remove the long thread (the 6-foot one). Then make two holes in the tower that has no windlass. Make a pencil-windlass and cut 2 notches in it. Slip this into the 2 holes and then repeat step 9. When you are finished, you will have a bridge with 2 windlasses, like the real lift bridge. However, you'll find that it isn't so easy to turn both windlasses at exactly the same speed. But whether you want 1 windlass or 2, you'll find that this bridge is easy to make and fun to work.

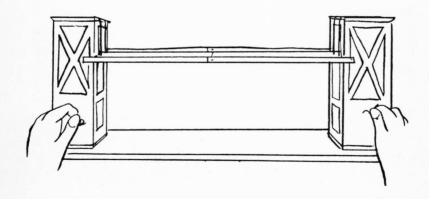

ARCH BRIDGES

Arch bridges can be seen over almost every river in the world. Some are brand-new, while others are thousands of years old. There are arch bridges made of stone, arch bridges made of wood, arch bridges made of steel— arch bridges everywhere you look. Why are arch bridges so popular?

One reason is that the arch form is quite beautiful, and people like to make things beautiful as well as useful. Another reason is that the arch form is strong, as you can see for yourself if you try this little experiment. All you need is a card, 2 books, a small dish or the lid of a tin can, and some pebbles (or other small, heavy objects).

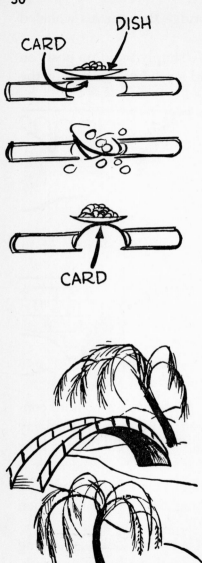

Lay the card across the books and place the dish on it. Then put pebbles into the dish, 1 or 2 at a time, until the card gives way completely and collapses. See how many pebbles were required to do the job.

Next, set the card in an arch form, propped against the books, and place the dish on top. Pile on the pebbles to see how many are needed to make the arch collapse. You'll find that the arched card can carry a heavier load, because it is stronger than a flat card.

Now let's look at a few kinds of arch bridges in use, and then we can get started on making a milk-carton model or two. Here's a picture of a small arch bridge over a little brooklet in a Japanese garden. It's very pretty, but it's also rather steep, too steep for cars or wagons to manage. We need a level roadway for an arch bridge that carries wheeled traffic.

And this is how we get it. We simply build up posts on top of the arch, and then build a roadway on top of the posts.

Or we can make the whole thing out of stone, like this.

Sometimes it is more convenient to hang the roadway *under* the arch. This is how it is done. First the arch is built. Then steel rods are attached to the arch. Then the roadway is fastened to the arch.

Notice that this type of arch bridge looks something like a hunter's bow. In fact, it is called a bowstring arch.

Now for the milk-carton model. This will be fairly easy to build. All you will need is 1 milk carton, a pencil, a ruler, a knife, and a dish (or pot lid).

1. Lay the dish across the milk carton, like this, and draw a curved line with a pencil.

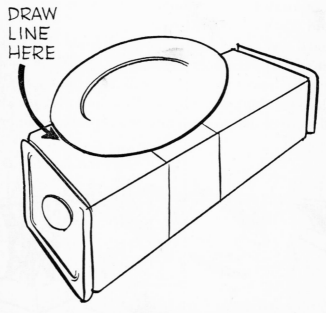

DRAW
LINE
HERE

2. Do the same thing on the opposite side of the carton.

3. Mark off the up-and-down lines as shown in the picture. Do this on both sides of the carton.

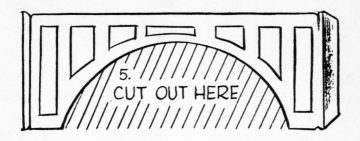

4. Cut off the paper between the lines.
5. Cut away the paper underneath the arch.

And that's all there is to it.

You'll find arch bridges so easy to build that you may want to make a whole series of them. When these are assembled end to end, you will have a repeated-arch bridge. This kind of bridge is often built over a wide but shallow river. Here's a picture of a repeated-arch bridge.

COVERED BRIDGES

This bridge looks like a house built over a river, and that's just about what it is. The floor of the house is the wooden roadway itself, while the walls and roof serve as protection. Wood, when it is wet, rots easily. So when the walls and roof keep off snow and rain, the bridge lasts longer. And, of course, a dry roadway is safer than a wet, slippery one, so there's another good reason for keeping the bridge covered.

Covered bridges made of wood were quite common 100 years ago, when steel and iron were expensive. Nowadays there are just a few left, mostly in New England, and no new ones are being built.

It's easy to build a milk-carton model of a covered bridge. All you will need is 2 milk cartons and 4 paper fasteners.

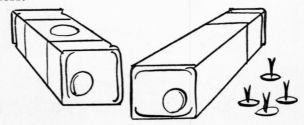

1. First, make the roadway and walls. Begin by cutting off the ends of one carton. Then cut a slit all across one side, from bottom to top.
   Then bend this cut side up into a slant.

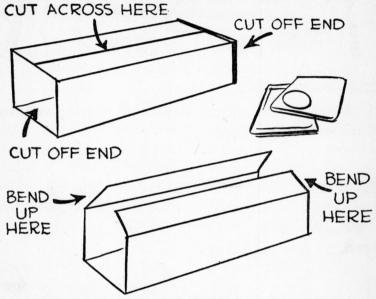

CUT ACROSS HERE

CUT OFF END

CUT OFF END

BEND UP HERE

BEND UP HERE

2. Now make the roof. Cut all the way down one side of a carton.
   Cut down the opposite side and across both ends.

CUT ALONG THIS CORNER

CUT ACROSS THE ENDS LIKE THIS

CUT ALONG THIS CORNER

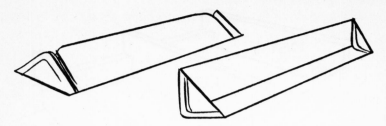

This will divide the carton into 2 halves. One half will
be the roof, while the other will be a spare in case you
need it.

3. With paper fasteners, attach the roof to the walls (as
shown in the picture).

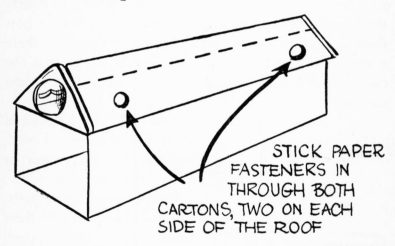

STICK PAPER
FASTENERS IN
THROUGH BOTH
CARTONS, TWO ON EACH
SIDE OF THE ROOF

And that's all—your covered bridge is finished.

That didn't take long, so let's spend some time looking
at a real covered bridge. It isn't built exactly like our
milk-carton model, of course, and the differences are
quite interesting. First, let's look at the floor, or roadway.

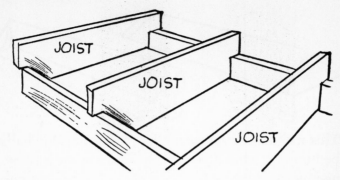

In the model it's just a flat piece of cardboard. In the real bridge it isn't just a flat sheet of lumber. Instead, we find long boards called joists underneath. These joists carry the weight of the roadway and the traffic. Notice how they are placed, resting on their narrow edges. Is there a special reason for this position, or is it just that the carpenter felt like doing it that way? Here is how you can find out.

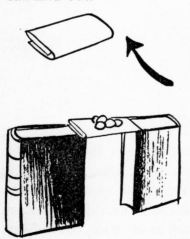

You will need 2 books of about the same size, 1 card, and some small stones or other heavy objects.

Fold the card in 3 parts.

Stand the books with their front edges facing each other, and rest the folded card across the top. Then pile on the stones one at a time and see what happens.

You will find that the card

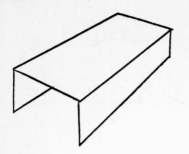

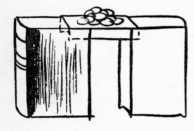

will bend under the weight of a few stones and then collapse completely.

Now unfold the card, so that it looks like the one in the picture. Slip it over the top of the books, between the covers, and pile on the stones once again. See what happens.

You will find that the card can carry a much greater weight than it did before. The card is much stronger when its sides are in an up-and-down position than when they are flat.

That's why the boards under a bridge—the joists—are mounted in an up-and-down position rather than in a flat one. They are stronger that way, and can carry a heavier load. For the same reason, the floor of your room is probably supported by joists in an up-and-down position. Don't go tearing up the floorboards to find out, because there's an easier way. Look at the ceiling of the cellar, and you'll probably see the boards that support the first-story floor. An attic, a barn, or a new building going up are other places where you can see this type of supporting structure.

And now, let's get back to bridges and milk cartons.

PONTOON BRIDGES

Probably you have never actually seen a pontoon bridge. You may have seen one in a movie. A pontoon bridge is usually a temporary affair, built to be used for a short time. It is thrown together to allow a group of men or vehicles to cross a river, and then it is taken apart. A pontoon bridge is really a string of boats fastened side to side, with a roadway of boards laid across the top.

You can build a milk-carton pontoon bridge in a few minutes. All you will need is several cartons, a large needle, and some thread or twine to fit the needle. The picture shows how to "sew" the cartons together in a row. The roadway itself is a board laid across the top.

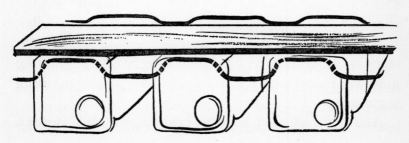

Your little pontoon bridge will be fine for carrying small-sized traffic, but don't try anything heavy on it. If you're interested in knowing how much it can carry, here's the answer. Each quart carton can hold just about 2 pounds without sinking. So, if you have 10 pontoon-cartons supporting your bridge, they have a lifting power of 20 pounds. If your board weighs, let's say, 3 pounds, that leaves 17 pounds for the heaviest possible weight of traffic. But better not load it that much unless you enjoy watching accidents!

SUSPENSION BRIDGES

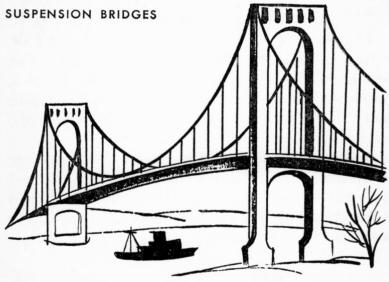

All the bridges you have learned about so far are quite small bridges, for crossing fairly narrow rivers. Now we come to the giants of the bridge family—the suspension bridge and the cantilever (căn'-tĭ-lē-ver) bridge. All the great bridges of the world are one or the other of these two types. Let's find out more about them. We'll begin with a suspension bridge. We are going to find out about suspension bridges by looking at a child's lemonade stand.

Here are some little children who have decided to set up a lemonade stand. In order to advertise the business, they hang up a sign on a bar or stick attached to a fence post. This doesn't work out well at all, because the weight of the sign causes the bar to bend.

How can the children keep the bar from bending? By attaching a string between the far end of the bar and the top of the post. The string pulls up the bar and keeps it from bending. Now the bar hangs down from, or is suspended from, the string.

Let's study the signpost a bit more. We find that it really consists of three parts. First there is the post that holds up the whole business, then there is the bar that carries the load, and then we have the string that holds up the far end of the bar.

Now if we took two such signposts and put them together, we'd have something that looks like this.

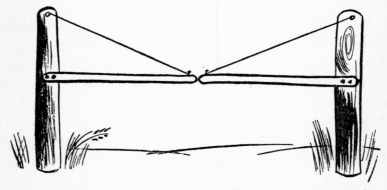

Notice how it resembles part of a suspension bridge.

A suspension bridge is really like 2 signposts joined end to end. There are 2 posts. These are like the 2 towers of the bridge. There are 2 bars, joined end to end. These make the roadway. And there are 2 strings joining the posts to the bars. These are the cables that support the roadway. And where is the sign itself? There is none, but instead there is the weight of the traffic that rolls and sways and pounds across the bridge.

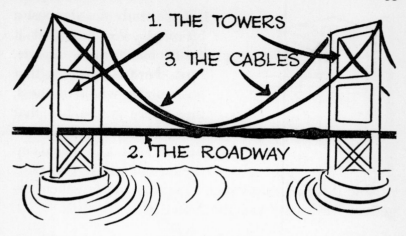

Now for your model bridge. You will need 4 milk cartons, about 8 feet of twine, a spool of thread, and 4 paper fasteners or a stapler and 8 tacks. You will also need a base for your bridge. This can be a piece of orange-crate wood or heavy corrugated paper, about 2 feet long and 4 inches wide.

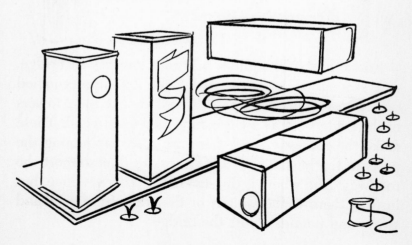

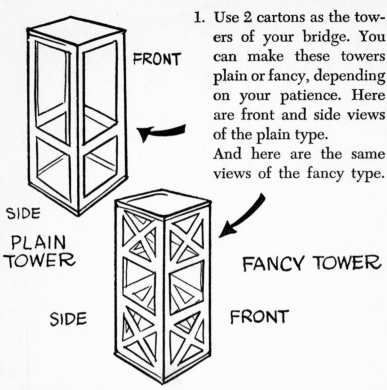

FRONT

SIDE

PLAIN TOWER

FANCY TOWER

SIDE   FRONT

1. Use 2 cartons as the towers of your bridge. You can make these towers plain or fancy, depending on your patience. Here are front and side views of the plain type.

And here are the same views of the fancy type.

2. After you have made the towers, fasten them to the base with 2 thumbtacks or staples in each tower.

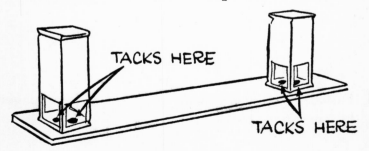

TACKS HERE

TACKS HERE

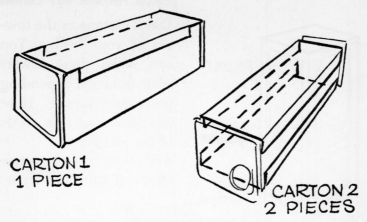

CARTON 1
1 PIECE

CARTON 2
2 PIECES

3. Now cut the roadway. This is made from the sides of 2 cartons, as shown in the picture

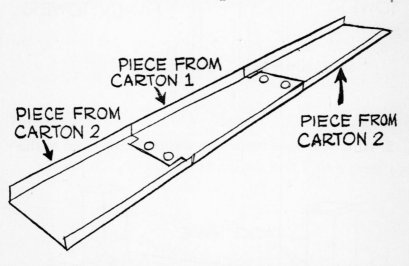

PIECE FROM
CARTON 1

PIECE FROM
CARTON 2

PIECE FROM
CARTON 2

4. Fasten the roadway strips end to end, using paper fasteners or staples.

NOTCH TO FIT INTO
TOWERS

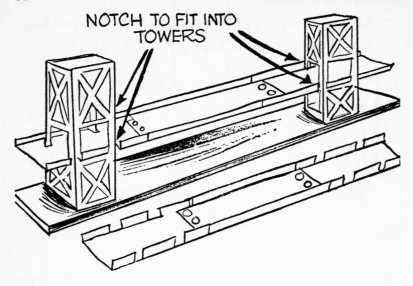

5. Set the roadway in place between the two towers. You will have to cut notches so the roadway will fit into the towers. Part of it will extend outward on each side.

6. Cut the twine into 2 pieces, each 4 feet long. These pieces will be the cables that hold up the roadway.

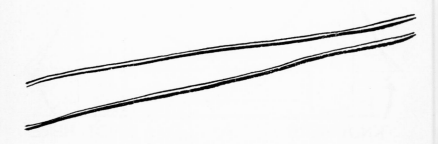

7. Make 2 holes at each end of the roadway, just large enough for the twine to pass through.

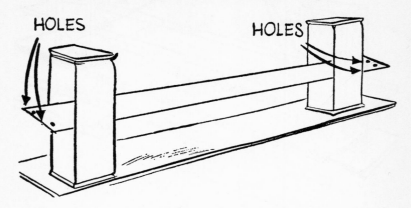

HOLES HOLES

8. Push an end of the twine through one of the holes and tie a knot. Loop the rest of the twine over one of the towers, then down toward the roadway, up over the other tower, and down to the roadway again. Finish off by passing the end of the twine through the hole in the roadway and tying a knot.

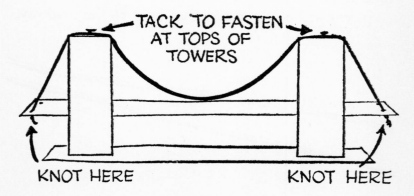

TACK TO FASTEN AT TOPS OF TOWERS

KNOT HERE   KNOT HERE

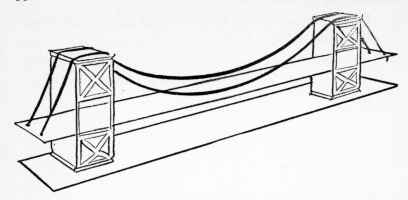

9. Repeat step 8 with the other piece of twine. Now you have a pair of cables for supporting the roadway of your suspension bridge.

10. Now for the last part, which takes some patience. Tie threads between the cables and roadway. Each thread has one end tied around a cable and the other end tied through a hole in the side of the roadway. The holes are made with the point of a compass. Make them about 2 inches apart, if you're in a hurry.

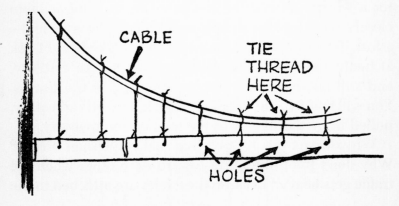

CABLE

TIE
THREAD
HERE

HOLES

But if you're willing to do a little more work, make the holes about 1 inch apart. Then you'll have more threads to tie, but your bridge will look more realistic. Here is how it should look when you are finished.

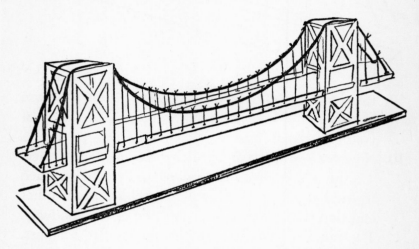

After you have gloated over your suspension bridge for a while, you may be interested in studying it more closely. Try this very simple experiment. Put a weight—a fork, for example—on the center of the roadway. Look at the towers. Then add another weight to the roadway, and still another, and see what happens to the towers. You will find that they begin to lean in toward each other, pulled in by the weight of the load on the roadway.

Why doesn't this happen to a real suspension bridge? Why don't the towers lean toward each other when the traffic gets heavy? Because the cables are attached to the river banks, or to tremendous blocks of concrete, at each end. The cables pull at the towers and keep them upright, holding the bridges steady. It's good that the engineers thought of it, isn't it?

CABLES
ATTACHED
HERE

Engineers have to think of lots of things when they design a bridge. One important thing is heat and cold. When metal is heated by the sun it expands, gets bigger. Cold causes metal to contract, to become smaller. The bigger a thing is, the more it expands when heated and the more it contracts when cooled. The long steel cables that hold up a big suspension bridge expand and contract quite a lot with changes in temperature. On a very hot summer day the cables are about 8 feet longer than on a very cold winter day.

This difference in length has to be taken into account when the bridge is designed. The roadway has to be made flexible, so that it can bend up slightly when the cables contract and bend down slightly when they expand. And the roadway needs room to expand and contract, too.

It probably will not surprise you to learn that a real suspension bridge is a bit harder to design and build than a milk-carton model of one! But in building your model, you have begun to get a tiny idea of the problems of the engineer and bridgebuilder.

CANTILEVER BRIDGES

Now let's work on the other member of the giant-bridge family—the cantilever bridge. Let's go back for a minute to the lemonade signpost we discussed in the chapter on suspension bridges. That signpost was made of a post, a bar, and a piece of string. The string was used to support the bar and keep it from bending.

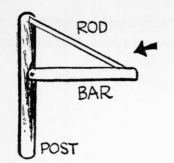

That same job could be done in another way, like this.

Notice that the bar is held up by a stiff rod, instead of a string.

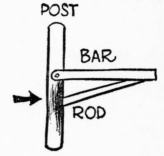

Or you could do the job this way, with a brace from the bottom.

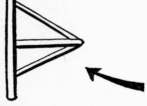

Or you could have a brace at the bottom and top, like this.

Now let's take any two such braced signposts and put them together. The result is a simple cantilever bridge. The posts are the towers. The bars, end to end, are the roadway. The braces are the rest of the bridge—the parts called struts and trusses and many other names.

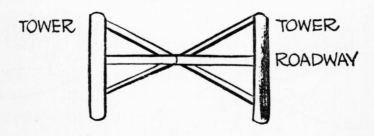

Real cantilever bridges are much more complicated, of course. But if we keep those signposts in mind we can see that cantilever bridges are of 3 main types.

1. The type with the braces underneath.
2. The type with the braces on top.
3. The type with the braces underneath and on top.

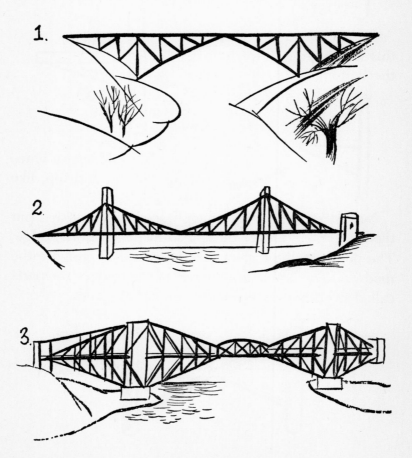

Not so complicated, after all! And now perhaps you'd like to build a milk-carton model of a cantilever bridge.

To build this model you will need 7 milk cartons, a base of orange-crate wood or corrugated cardboard 2½ feet long and about 4 inches wide, 4 thumbtacks, and about 3 dozen paper fasteners. If you have a stapler you won't need the fasteners.

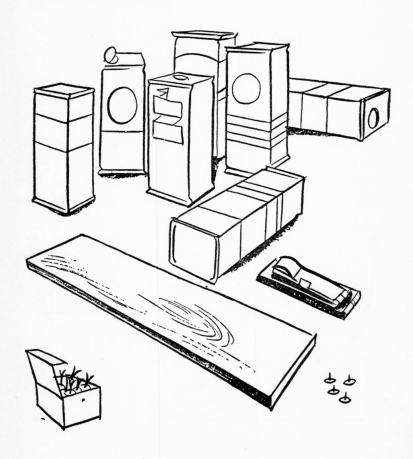

1. First, make the 2 towers. As with the suspension bridge, you can make the towers plain or fancy. Here are pictures of both types.

2. Now for the span. Cut apart 4 cartons, on a slant, as the picture shows. Then cut off the ends. When you're finished cutting, you will have 8 pieces that look like this.

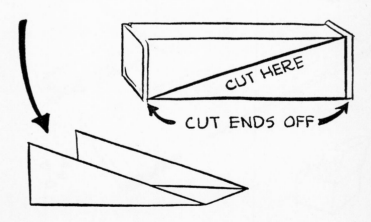

CUT HERE

CUT ENDS OFF

3. Each one of these pieces gets the same treatment—you cut triangle-shaped parts out of it until it looks like this.

4. Now for the center span. This is really a little bridge by itself, held in place by the rest of the bridge. Not all cantilever bridges have this kind of center, but you may as well build one for your model. It doesn't take long and it makes your model look a lot more real. Just cut away the top and bottom and one side of a carton, like this.

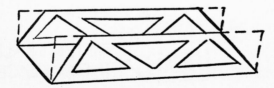

5. Then cut away triangle-shaped pieces until it looks like this.

Now you're all set for assembling your Milk-carton Super-special Cantilever Bridge. (It needs such a big name because it's quite an impressive-looking structure.) You assemble it with paper fasteners or staples, depending on what you have handy. Paper fasteners have a nice, shiny look, like real rivets, but staples are quicker to use. Here are the steps for assembling:

1. Fasten 2 roadway pieces back to back. Do this with all eight of the roadway pieces, so that you have 4 double pieces.

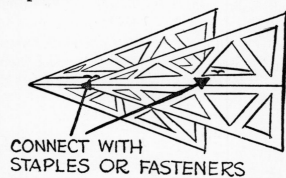

CONNECT WITH STAPLES OR FASTENERS

2. With paper fasteners or staples, attach the double pieces to the towers.

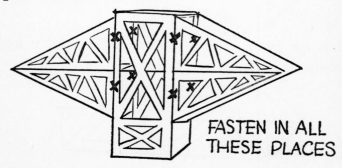

FASTEN IN ALL THESE PLACES

3. Attach each tower to the base, using thumbtacks or paper fasteners. The towers should be just far enough apart to permit the center span to fit in place nicely.

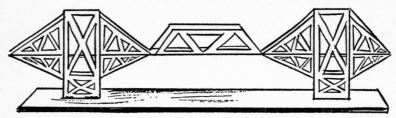

4. Attach the center span to the rest of the bridge, and you're done with the major part.

5. If you want your bridge to look even better than it already does, put on some cross bracing. This is used on real bridges to keep them from swaying too much in a strong wind. To make cross bracing, cut the sides from 2 milk cartons, like this. This will give you 4 trough-shaped pieces.

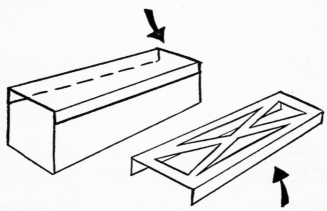

6. Cut triangles out of each piece, like this.

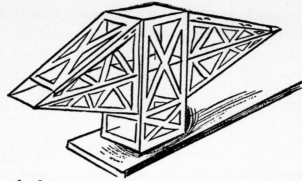

7. Attach the pieces to the top part of the cantilevers, using paper fasteners or staples, and you're done.

Handsome, isn't it? And quite strong, too! Try riding some toy trucks or trains across it, to test its strength.

Perhaps you'd like to design some bridge models yourself. After all, if you have been building these models one after the other, you've had quite a bit of practice. So here are sketches of two different types of cantilever bridges. See if you can design them down to milk-carton size. Have fun!

ROLLING ALONG

OXCARTS

PERHAPS YOU have seen the automobile advertisement that describes "the latest thing on wheels." Well, here you have the "earliest thing on wheels."

Oxcarts have been in use for thousands of years, and were probably the first wheeled vehicles ever invented.

You can make a milk-carton model of an oxcart in a few minutes.

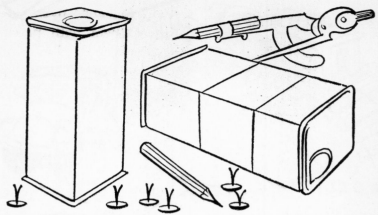

You will need 2 clean, rinsed cartons, 6 paper fasteners, a pencil, and a compass.

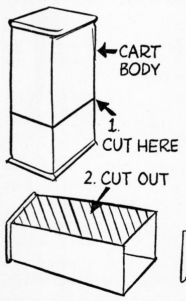

←CART BODY

1.
CUT HERE

2. CUT OUT

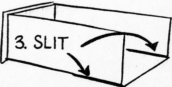

3. SLIT

1. Draw a line 5½ inches from the bottom all around one carton. Then cut along this line. Your carton is now in 2 pieces. The longer one will be the body of the cart.

2. Cut away one complete side of the body.

3. Then cut a 2-inch slit down each of the edges.

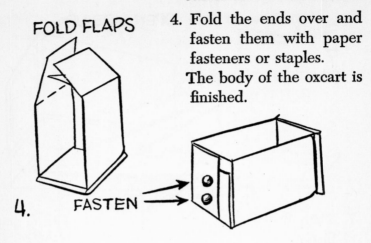

FOLD FLAPS

4. Fold the ends over and fasten them with paper fasteners or staples.
The body of the oxcart is finished.

4.   FASTEN

5. Now for the frame. From the other carton cut a piece shaped like this.

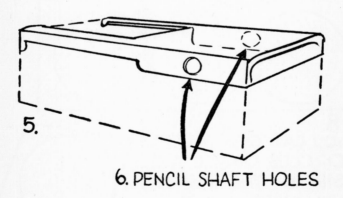

5.

6. PENCIL SHAFT HOLES

6. Bore 2 holes for the pencil shaft. These holes should be large enough to permit the shaft to turn freely.

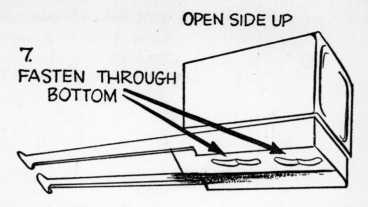

OPEN SIDE UP

7.
FASTEN THROUGH
BOTTOM

7. Then fasten the body to the frame with 2 paper fasteners.

8. To make the wheels, set your compass points 1¼ inches apart and draw 4 circles.

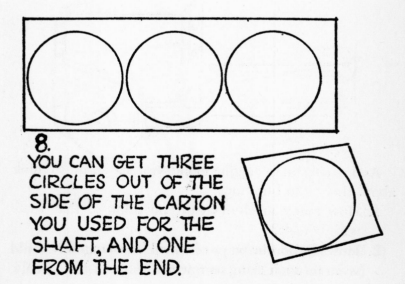

8.
YOU CAN GET THREE
CIRCLES OUT OF THE
SIDE OF THE CARTON
YOU USED FOR THE
SHAFT, AND ONE
FROM THE END.

9. Cut out these circles and fasten them, 2 together, to make 2 double-thick wheels.

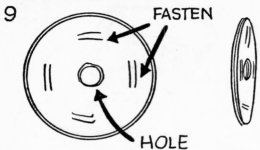

10. Bore a hole in each wheel, barely large enough for a tight squeeze of your pencil.
11. Mount the wheels and shaft on the frame of your oxcart, and you're all set. Have a good trip!

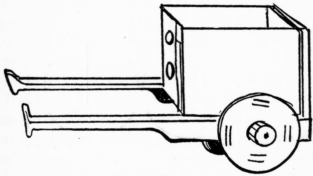

And while you're jogging along, you may want to think about these two questions:

1. How many machines can you think of that work with wheels?
2. How would our ways of travel be changed if there were no such thing as a wheel?

DUMP TRUCKS

A truck is an important part of everyday building and carting operations. A dump truck has one big advantage over an ordinary truck. Its load can be dumped without having to be shoveled out by hand. To get this done, it is necessary for the body of the truck to be raised high enough for the load to slide out down a chute or fall through an open tail gate. You have probably seen the coal trucks whose bodies are lifted high up by "piston lifters," like the ones in the picture.

The tilting dump truck is the kind used for transporting sand, soil, rocks, and many other materials. You can see these trucks scurrying about, dumping their loads wherever a new building is going up or a new road or bridge is being built.

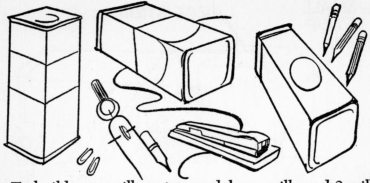

To build your milk-carton model you will need 3 milk cartons, 3 pencils, 2 hairpins or paper clips, a compass, 1 or 2 feet of string, and paper fasteners or a stapler.

1. First, let's build the frame or chassis (pronounced shassee). Cut one carton in half the long way.

CUT HERE

2. Now for the hood of the motor. This is made of 2 strips of milk-carton paper. One strip makes the sides and top, and the other strip makes the front. Fold the larger strip in a U shape and fasten it to the frame. Then fold the smaller strip in an L shape and fasten it to the front of the frame.

LARGE STRIP   **SMALL STRIP**

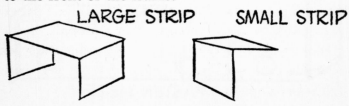

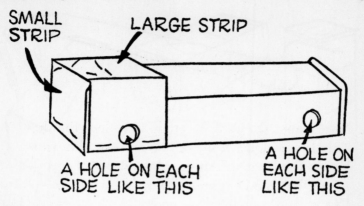

SMALL STRIP

LARGE STRIP

A HOLE ON EACH SIDE LIKE THIS

A HOLE ON EACH SIDE LIKE THIS

3. Bore 4 holes—2 in front of the chassis, and 2 in back. These holes are for the pencils that will act as wheel shafts, so bore them large enough for the pencils to turn freely in them.

4. The driver of the truck will need protection from the wind and rain, so let's build a cab to cover him. This is a simple job, as the picture shows. After you have cut it, fasten it in place.

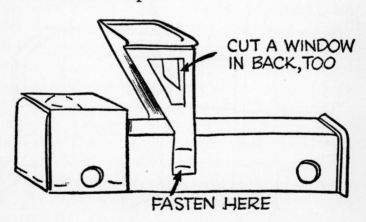

CUT A WINDOW IN BACK, TOO

FASTEN HERE

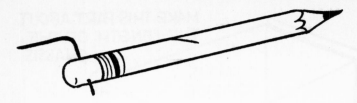

5. Next comes the little machine that does the dumping. This is a pencil-windlass, like the one that raises and lowers the bascule bridge. Make it out of a pencil and a bent hairpin or paper clip, as shown in the picture. Cut a small notch in the center of the pencil. (Later you will slip the end of a piece of string into this notch.) Bore 2 holes in the sides of the chassis and slip your pencil-windlass into the holes.

PENCIL WINDLASS
GOES HERE

6. Now for the body of your dump truck. This is made out of a milk carton with one end cut off. The tail gate is a strip of milk-carton paper cut to size and held in place by a straightened-out hairpin or paper clip. To

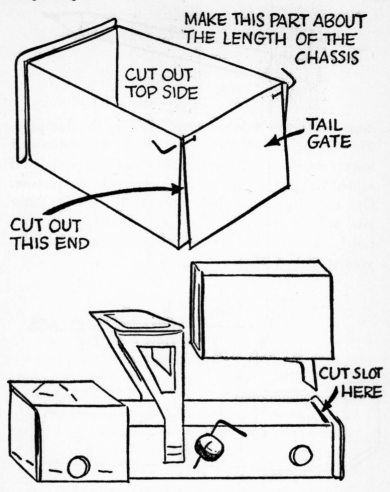

MAKE THIS PART ABOUT
THE LENGTH OF THE
CHASSIS

CUT OUT
TOP SIDE

TAIL
GATE

CUT OUT
THIS END

CUT SLOT
HERE

hold the body in place on the chassis, cut a small strip
of paper and bend it into an L shape. Fasten one end
of it to the bottom of the body. The other end will fit
into a slot cut into the end of the chassis.

7. Now you're ready to attach the pencil-windlass to the body of the truck. First make 3 small holes—1 in the top of the cab, 1 in the chassis directly beneath it, and 1 at the front bottom of the body.

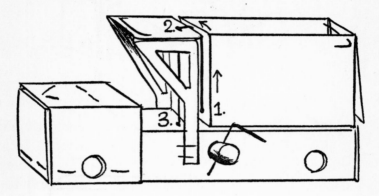

Pass one end of the string through the hole in the body and tie a large bumpy knot that will keep it from slipping out. Then pass the other end of the string first through the hole in the top of the cab, then through the hole in the chassis, and then through the notch in the pencil-windlass.

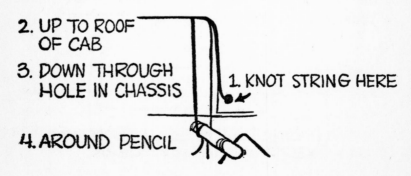

2. UP TO ROOF OF CAB

3. DOWN THROUGH HOLE IN CHASSIS

1. KNOT STRING HERE

4. AROUND PENCIL

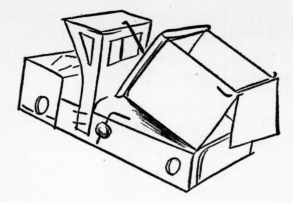

Turn the crank of the windlass until you have wound up all slack of the string. Now if you wind a little further, you will see the body tilt up, ready to dump its load. Turn the windlass the other way, and the body will settle back into place. '

8. Now for the wheels. Set your compass points 1 inch apart and draw 8 circles. Cut out the circles and staple them together in pairs. Bore a hole in the center of each wheel, just large enough to make a very tight fit for the pencil shafts. Push the shafts into the holes in the chassis. Then force the wheels onto the shafts. Your dump truck is finished!

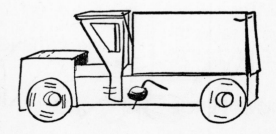

MOTOR CRANES

Now that your dump truck is finished, you'll want to load it in professional style. Here is the machine that will do it for you. This model motor crane can go through the motions of a real one. It rolls along the ground, its body swivels around, its boom moves up and down when you turn a crank, and its little bucket rides up and down when you turn still another crank.

To build your model, you will need 3 milk cartons, 4 pencils, 2 hairpins, 2 pieces of string (each 1 foot long), a paper clip, a paper fastener, and a stapler (if you have one).

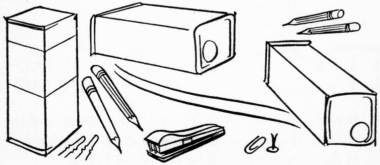

1. First, build the frame (or chassis). This is just like the one you made for the dump truck. Simply cut a carton lengthwise.

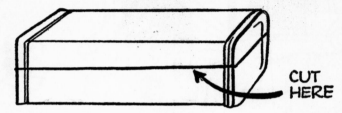

CUT
HERE

2. Now make the motor hood out of 2 strips of milk-carton paper. One strip is folded into a U shape and stapled to the sides of the frame. The other is L-shaped and stapled to the front.

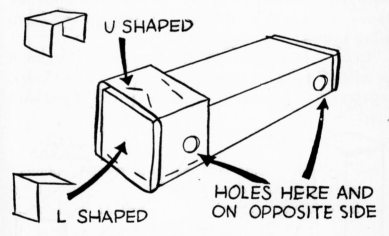

U SHAPED

L SHAPED

HOLES HERE AND
ON OPPOSITE SIDE

3. Bore 2 holes near the front and 2 near the rear of the chassis. Make these just large enough for a loose fit of the pencils that will be the wheel shafts.

4. Now you're ready for the driver's cab. This is a 1-piece job, made just like the one for the dump truck, and fastened into place with staples or paper fasteners.

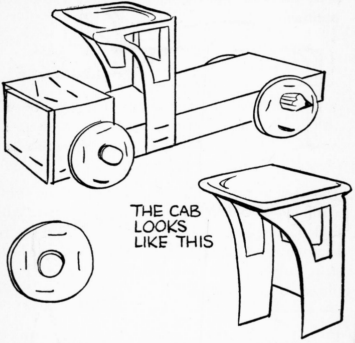

THE CAB
LOOKS
LIKE THIS

5. The wheels come next. Set your compass points ½ inch apart and draw 8 circles. Cut them out and fasten them together in pairs. They are stronger that way. Bore a hole in the center of each wheel, just large enough for a very tight fit of the pencils. Then slip the pencils into the holes in the chassis and force the wheels on.

6. Now you are ready to make the hoisting machinery. The housing for the machinery comes first. This housing is a milk carton cut in half, crosswise. Cut a narrow piece off one side, as in the picture. This will make room to allow the boom to rise to a straight-up position.

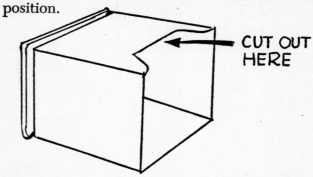

CUT OUT HERE

7. The boom is made of 2 strips of paper. Each strip is a full-length corner cut from a milk carton. When folded, each strip will be 1 inch wide and the full length of a carton. Bore a hole near one end of each strip, large enough for a loose fit of pencil. Fasten the other ends together.

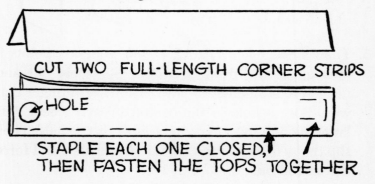

CUT TWO FULL-LENGTH CORNER STRIPS

HOLE

STAPLE EACH ONE CLOSED, THEN FASTEN THE TOPS TOGETHER

8. Prepare 2 pencil-windlasses, each with a handle made of a bent hairpin or paper clip, and with a notch in the middle for fastening a piece of string.

9. Bore 2 pairs of holes in the machinery housing. One pair is low down, near the back end, and the other pair is high up, near the front.

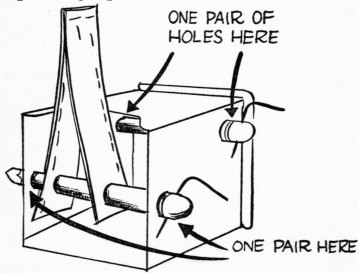

ONE PAIR OF HOLES HERE

ONE PAIR HERE

10. Set the boom into place and push one of the pencil-windlasses through to hold it in place. Push the other pencil-windlass through the holes in the front end of the housing.

11. Tie one end of a string to the boom. Make a small hole in the top of the housing and pass the other end of the string through this hole and slip it into the notch of the rear pencil-windlass.

When you turn the handle one way, the boom will rise. When you turn it the other way, the boom goes down.

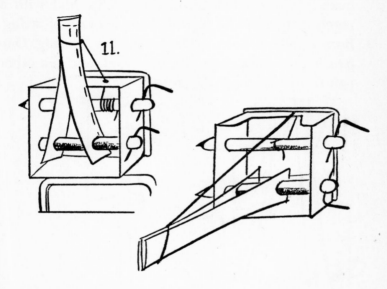

12. Slide a paper clip onto the high end of the boom. Then pass a string through the clip and fasten one end by slipping it into the notch in the front pencil-windlass.

13. Make a little box out of milk-carton paper and attach it to the string.

14. To attach the machinery housing to the chassis, make a small hole in the middle of the floor of the housing. Make another hole in the chassis, right under the hole in the housing.

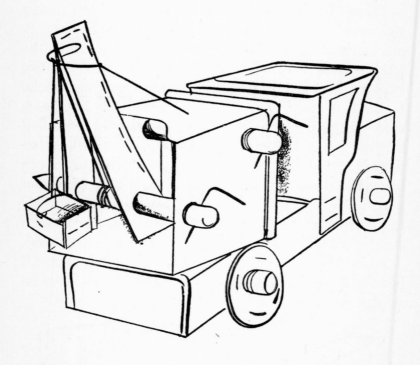

Slip a paper fastener through both holes, bend apart the ends of the fastener, and you're all set. The Super De Luxe Hoisting Company is ready for business.

TRAILER TRUCKS

These "freight cars of the highways" are a familiar sight everywhere. As their name tells you, they are a 2-piece affair. The trailer part carries the cargo, while the truck carries the engine and the driver. There are two important reasons for building them in 2 separate pieces. In the first place, they can turn a narrow corner much more easily than a single long truck can (you will find this out for yourself after you build your milk-carton model). Secondly, they are timesavers. The driver can bring a load to a factory or warehouse, jack up the trailer part, and leave it to be unloaded. Then he can drive away in the truck part and pick up another loaded trailer, instead of waiting around for the first trailer to be unloaded.

To build your model you will need 3 milk cartons, 3 pencils, 5 paper fasteners, and a stapler. If you have no stapler, you will need about 2 dozen paper fasteners.

1. The truck frame or chassis is made by slicing a carton lengthwise.

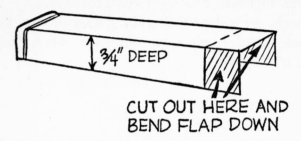

¾" DEEP

CUT OUT HERE AND
BEND FLAP DOWN

2. Make a cab for the driver, just like the ones you made for the dump truck and the motor crane. Fasten it to the side of the chassis.

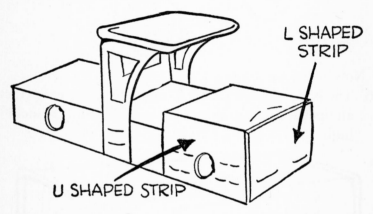

L SHAPED
STRIP

U SHAPED STRIP

3. Make a hood for the motor out of 2 strips of paper. This is made in the same way as the hood for the dump truck.

4. Bore holes in the sides of the chassis, large enough for a loose fit of the pencils.

5. To make the wheels, set your compass points ¾ inch apart and draw 12 circles. Cut them out and fasten them together two by two. This will give you 6 wheels, 4 for the truck and 2 for the trailer. Put the truck wheels in place on their axles. That completes the truck part.

Now make the trailer.

6. The body of the trailer is a complete milk carton. Cut an opening in one side, 4 inches wide and 2¼ inches high.

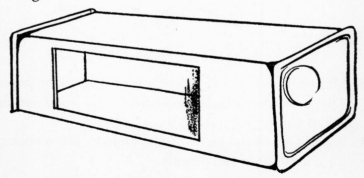

7. Cut 2 doors from a piece of milk carton. Each door is 2½ inches wide and 2½ inches high. Push a paper fastener into each, to act as a doorknob.

8. Now we make the grooves in which the doors slide. These are made by cutting 2 corners from a carton. Each corner is the full length of the carton and about ¼ inch wide. Fasten these corners to the truck body, one at the bottom and one at the top. Set the doors in place in the grooves.

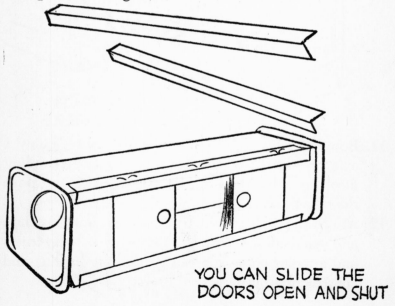

YOU CAN SLIDE THE DOORS OPEN AND SHUT

9. The chassis of the trailer is made by cutting a carton lengthwise, and cutting away one end, leaving you a piece 6 inches long and ¾ inch deep.

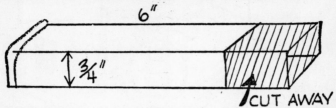

CUT AWAY

10. With 2 paper fasteners, attach the body of the trailer to its chassis.

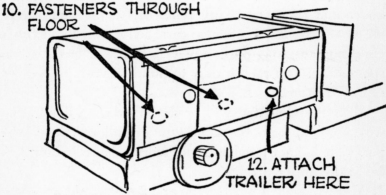

10. FASTENERS THROUGH FLOOR

12. ATTACH TRAILER HERE

11. Bore holes for the axle of the trailer (there's only 1 axle). Make the hole big enough for an easy-rolling fit of the axle. Then set the axle in place and push the wheels on.

12. Attach the trailer to the truck with a paper fastener, and you're all set. With a trailer truck, a dump truck, and a motor crane you can go into the hauling and construction business.

RAIL-CAR UNDERCARRIAGES

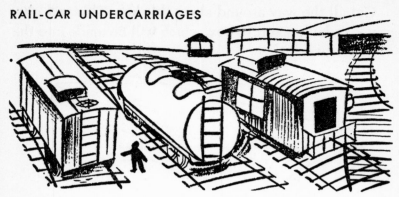

If you have ever visited a railroad freight yard, you know that there are many types of freight cars. There are coal cars, flatcars, cattle cars, refrigerator cars, tank cars, boxcars, and dozens of others. Each has its own special use. And each is easy to build—if you build it out of milk cartons.

All the models that will be described are alike in one way. They all have the same type of undercarriage (the part that holds the wheels and axles). Here is how you build the undercarriage.

1. You will need a milk carton and 2 pencils. Draw a line down one side of the carton, 1 inch from the corner. Do the same on the other side and on the top and bottom.

Cut all the way around along this line. This will give you a shallow sort of box, which will be made into the undercarriage.

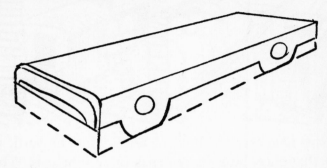

Now cut the sides of the box into this shape. Then bore holes for the axles, and you're finished.

2. The wheels are made in the same way as the truck wheels, but set your compass points ½ inch apart. You can find directions on page 94.

After you have set the wheels and axles in place, the undercarriage is complete.

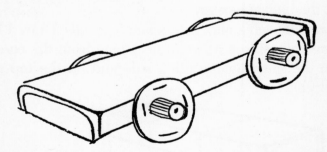

Now you are ready to build several types of freight cars.

FLATCARS

A flatcar is a floor on wheels. It is used for carrying very large pieces of freight, too large to fit in through the doors of a closed freight car.

You have probably seen flatcars carrying large machines, trucks, and other bulky things.

To build your milk-carton flatcar you will need— nothing at all. You have already built it. The undercarriage described on the previous page will do fine as a flatcar. So now you have car number 1 of the Milk-carton Special, all ready to roll.

GONDOLAS

Gondolas are used for carrying coal, sand, and other loose materials that pour easily. The open top makes a gondola easy to load and unload, but it also exposes the cargo to rain and snow. You will never see sugar or salt being carried in a gondola.

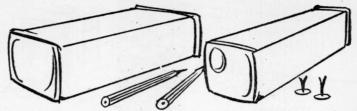

To build the gondola of the Milk-carton Special, you will need 2 cartons, 2 pencils, and 2 paper fasteners.

First build the undercarriage, as described on page 104. Then cut away one side of a carton. Attach it to the undercarriage with 2 paper fasteners. Freight car number 2 is ready.

BOXCARS

This is the most common type of freight car. It has a top to protect its cargo from rain and snow. It has doors that can be locked to protect its cargo from people not as honest as you.

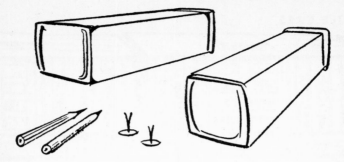

You will need 2 cartons, 2 pencils, and 2 paper fasteners.

Directions for building the undercarriage are on pages 104–105.

The body of the boxcar is built like the body of the trailer truck. You will find directions on pages 101–103.

Attach the body to the undercarriage with 2 paper fasteners. You push these through the floor of the body and the undercarriage.

Now freight car number 3 is ready to roll.

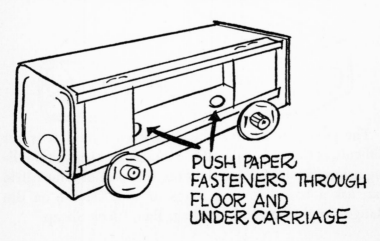

PUSH PAPER
FASTENERS THROUGH
FLOOR AND
UNDER CARRIAGE

CATTLE CARS

Cattle cars are used for carrying—you guessed it—cattle. A cattle car is similar to a boxcar, except that its sides are built of slats to let in air and light.

When loaded, it also lets out moos or baas, depending upon the type of cattle it is carrying.

All you will have to get are 2 cartons, 2 pencils, and 2 paper fasteners. But you will also need something else, a fair amount of patience.

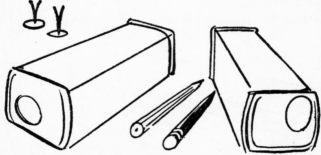

The job of cutting out the slats, even though it is not difficult, is rather boring after a while. To keep from falling asleep while you are building this part of your cattle car, ask a friend to sing songs to you. "Home on the Range" might be good, or "Baa, Baa, Black Sheep."

The body of the cattle car is the same as the body of the trailer truck. You will find directions on pages 101–103.

To cut the slats in the cattle car, first cut a piece of thick cardboard about 3 inches long and 2 inches wide. Slip this inside the carton and hold it against the side. It will support the place where you are cutting.

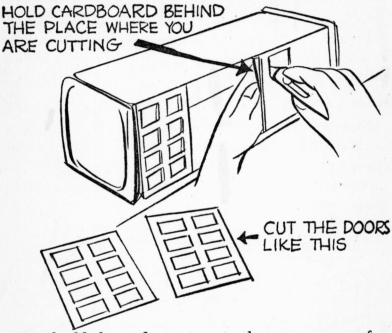

HOLD CARDBOARD BEHIND THE PLACE WHERE YOU ARE CUTTING

CUT THE DOORS LIKE THIS

You build the undercarriage in the same way as for the other freight-car models.

Attach the body to the undercarriage with 2 paper fasteners. You push these through the floor of the body and the undercarriage.

Freight car number 4 is ready to roll. If you want it to look very much like the real thing, try loading it with a cargo of toy animals. Or even better, some live mice.

MORE CARS FOR YOUR TRAIN

Now you have a flatcar, a gondola, a boxcar, and a cattle car. As you built them, you probably had ideas for other types of railroad cars, too.

Now is a good time for you to try building some. Here are pictures of several kinds.

Can you design models of these cars? Have fun!

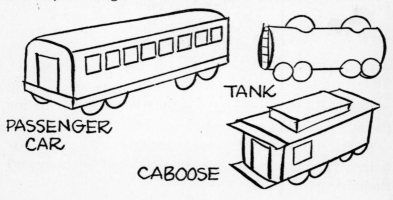

PASSENGER CAR

TANK

CABOOSE

SAILING ALONG

CANALS AND CANAL LOCKS

HERE IS a city ten miles from the sea. There are many factories in the city, making all kinds of machinery. Much of the machinery is sent to other countries, across the sea.

The machinery is loaded on freight cars, carried to the harbor, unloaded from the freight cars, and then at last, loaded on ships. First on, then off, and then on again—lots of work and trouble. If the ships could sail right up to the city, there would be only one loading job instead of three.

How can this be done?

A canal can do it for us. If we dig a canal from the sea to the city, the ships can sail all the way in. Then no

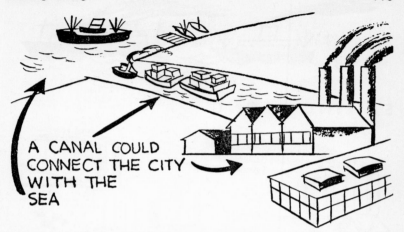

A CANAL COULD CONNECT THE CITY WITH THE SEA

extra loading and lifting will be needed. So far, everything looks fine.

But there's an "if" to the plan. If the land between the city and the sea is level, the plan will work. Water will flow in and fill the canal. The ships can sail on the canal.

But if the city is higher than the sea, what then? Water will not flow uphill from the sea to the city. A sloping canal will not work.

But we can divide the whole canal into several short canals, one after the other. Each is higher than the one before, like a series of wide steps.

Each short canal can be level.

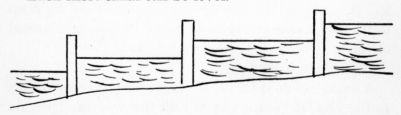

What we need now is a way of carrying the ships up or down from one step to the next.

A canal lock can do the job. A canal lock can raise a ship from one canal to another higher up. Or it can lower the ship from the higher canal to the lower. Let's see how it works.

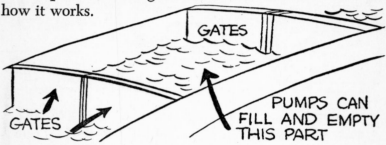

A canal lock is two huge pairs of gates, built across a canal. The gates are opened and closed by electric motors. One pair of gates is built across the end of the higher canal. The other is built across the lower canal.

The part of the canal between the two pairs of gates can be filled with water or emptied. Big pumps do the job.

Here you see a ship in the lower canal. The lower gates have been opened and the ship is sailing into the lock.

Now both pairs of gates are closed. Water is being pumped into the space between the two pairs of gates.

As the water fills the space, the ship is lifted higher and higher.

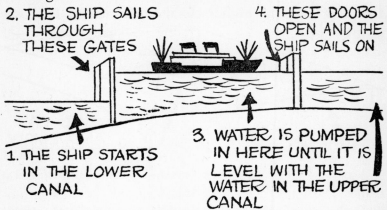

2. THE SHIP SAILS THROUGH THESE GATES

4. THESE DOORS OPEN AND THE SHIP SAILS ON

1. THE SHIP STARTS IN THE LOWER CANAL

3. WATER IS PUMPED IN HERE UNTIL IT IS LEVEL WITH THE WATER IN THE UPPER CANAL

When the water has risen high enough, the upper pair of gates is opened, and the ship sails out into the upper canal. The job is done.

Let's suppose that another ship comes along in the other direction. It has to be brought from the higher canal down to the lower.

Can you work out the way to do it?

Begin with this picture which shows the upper gates open, the lower gates closed, and the water in the lock at a high level.

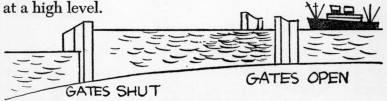

GATES SHUT

GATES OPEN

The answer is down below in the next paragraph, but first try to work it out for yourself.

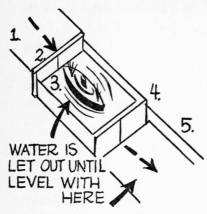

1.

2.

3.

4.

5.

WATER IS
LET OUT UNTIL
LEVEL WITH
HERE

These are the steps for lowering a ship:

1. Ship enters the lock.
2. Upper gates are closed. (Lower gates are already closed.)
3. Water is let out from the space between the upper and lower gates.
4. Lower gates are opened.
5. Ship leaves the lock.

Now that you have sent the ship on its way, here's another problem to work out. A canal lock can handle one large ship at a time, or two or more smaller ones. Suppose that a small ship in the upper canal is waiting to go down,

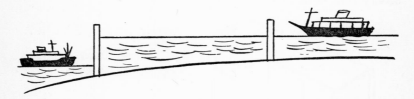

and another small ship in the lower canal is waiting to go up. Can the lock handle both ships at the same time?

If you have worked out the correct answer (which is No) you can understand why some busy canals have two sets of locks. Upstream ships use one lock and downstream ships use the other.

A canal lock at work is very interesting to watch. Perhaps you're lucky enough to live near enough to one to pay a visit. Here are the locations of some canal locks in this country: there are fifty-seven locks in the New York State Barge Canal between Troy and Buffalo. There are fifty on the Ohio River between Pittsburgh, Pennsylvania, and Cairo, Illinois. There are locks on the New Orleans Industrial Canal in Louisiana, on the Lake Washington Ship Canal in Washington State, and on many other rivers and canals.

Here's another way of watching a canal lock at work—build your own out of milk cartons!

It will take only a few minutes to build a simple, leaky canal lock. It will take much time and patience to build one with snug-fitting gates that hold water. Just for practice, let's build the simple, leaky one first.

You will need 2 rinsed milk cartons and a stapler. Cut away one side of one of the cartons.

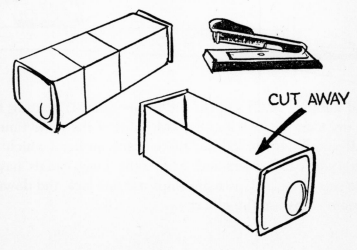

CUT AWAY

From the other carton cut 4 gates. Each gate is 2¾ inches high (the width of your carton). It is 2 inches wide. Fold each along the dotted line, as shown in the picture.

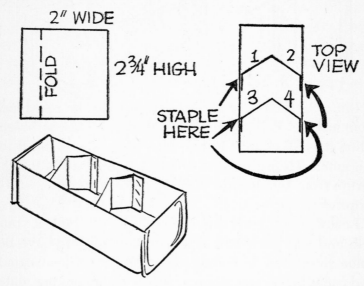

Now staple the gates in place in the carton "canal," and you are done.

Try out your leaky canal lock with a chip of wood as the ship. Practice the steps in raising and lowering a ship. Don't be discouraged if the lock doesn't hold water long enough to go through all the steps.

You can even practice the steps without water and with imagination.

Building a good canal lock calls for more care and patience. The gates have to fit very snugly.

A strip of felt will help them to fit well. Staple the felt along the bent "hinge," at the bottom, and along the edge where the two gates meet.

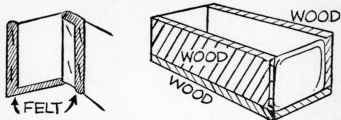

But even the felt is not enough to keep the canal lock from leaking. Perhaps you noticed that the carton bulges when it is filled with water. This bulge spoils the fit of the gates. To prevent the bulge, you have to brace the carton from the outside. Above is a way to do it with 3 strips of wood.

Leaky or not, you have a canal lock. You built it yourself, and you know how it works. Perhaps you have become interested in finding out more about real canals and canal locks. You will find plenty of interesting material in almost any encyclopedia.

CANAL BOATS

Now that you have a canal lock, you will want a canal boat. The one described here is easy to build. It is too big, however, to fit into your canal lock. You can build a smaller boat that will fit, but it is a little harder work. Let's do the big one, in any case.

You will need 2 milk cartons, a paper clip, and a stapler or 6 paper fasteners.

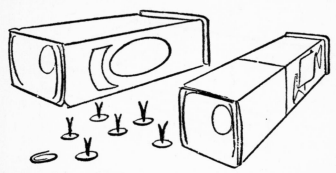

First make the main part of the boat—the part called the hull.

On one carton, mark a line 1¼ inches from one edge, all the way around the carton. Then cut through this line. Now your hull is done.

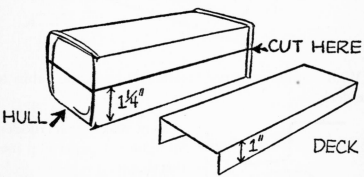

Next comes the deck. Cut a piece shaped like the hull, but only 1 inch deep.

Cut away each end. The deck is finished.

Now for the cabin. Cut a piece just like the deck. Then cut and fold it like this.

Cut along the solid lines and fold along the dotted lines.

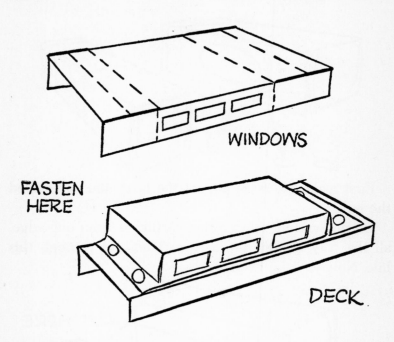

WINDOWS

FASTEN HERE

DECK

With staples or paper fasteners, attach the cabin to the deck.

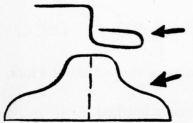

Now make your rudder. Straighten a paper clip into this shape.

Cut a piece of carton into this shape.

Fold it in half.

Attach it to the paper clip with staples or paper fasteners. Now your rudder is finished.

Now you need a hinge for the rudder. Cut a piece like this.

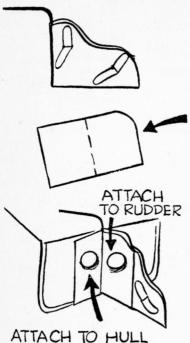

Attach it to the rudder with staples or paper fasteners. Then attach the other side of the hinge to the hull.

Now put the deck and cabin into the hull, and you're all set. Your Colossal Canal Cruiser is ready for business.

ATTACH TO RUDDER

ATTACH TO HULL

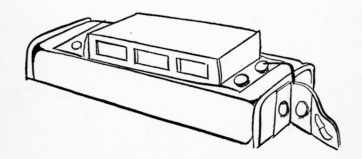

HOUSEBOATS

This boat is very easy to build. All you will need is 1 milk carton.

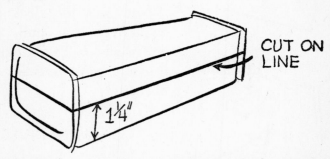

CUT ON LINE

1¼"

First cut the hull. This is made in the same way as the hull of the canal boat.

Then cut the fore and aft decks. Each is a piece 4 inches long and 1½ inches wide. Cut them so as to make use of the folds in the carton.

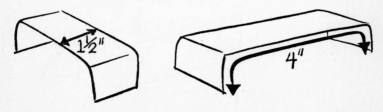

1½"

4"

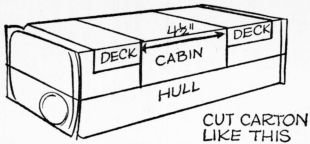

CUT CARTON
LIKE THIS

The cabin is a piece 6 inches long and 4½ inches wide. This, too, should be cut so as to make use of the folds in the carton.

Bend the cabin piece into a curve. An easy way to do this is to pull it across the edge of a table.

Now put the cabin and the two decks into the hull. Your houseboat is ready to sail.

After you have built the canal boat and houseboat, you may like to design other milk-carton boats yourself. You can find pictures in the encyclopedia and in books about boats. Have fun!

GOING UP!

GOING DOWN!

ELEVATORS

THIS LITTLE elevator model is easy to build. After you have made it, you may want to inspect the machinery of a real elevator, with the building superintendent as a guide. When you do, you will discover some important differences between the real thing and your model. But your model will really work too

You will need 1 complete milk carton, and some large scraps of milk cartons left over from one of your previous projects. You will also need a pencil, a hairpin or paper clip, 1 foot of thread, a spool, and a stapler or 4 paper fasteners.

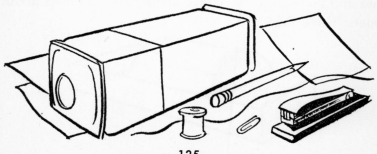

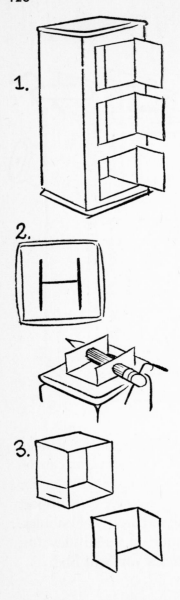

1. Cut 3 elevator doors in one side of the carton. Each door is 2¼ inches high.

2. Cut a large H in the bottom of the carton. (By the way, the bottom of the carton will be the top of your elevator. This is an upside-down job.) Then bend up the sides of the H and bore a hole in each side. The hole should permit a loose fit of the pencil. Put the bent hairpin through the eraser for a handle.

3. Make an elevator car out of milk-carton paper. This car is really a box held sideways. You can make it out of 2 pieces, one shaped like a square O and the other like a U, as in the picture. Make sure the car is small enough to fit into the elevator shaft, through one door.

Fasten the O and U pieces together with staples or paper fasteners. Then bore a hole in the top center and push a string through. Tie a match to the string and then you're ready to install the car in its shaft.

4. Put the car into the shaft. Pass the string up through the top of the shaft and wrap it twice around the pencil. Then tie it to the spool.

Now you're ready to go into business as the Eureka Vertical Transportation Company. This elevator can be a pleasant little surprise gift for a younger child or for the kindergarten class. It is strong enough to transport little dolls or small wooden animals or cargoes of pebbles.

Try to arrange for a guided tour of a real elevator. Here are some important differences you will find.

MOTOR

CABLES

COUNTER-
WEIGHT

1. The counterweight on your model is a spool, while on the real elevator it is a stack of iron slabs.

2. Your model works from the top, where you turn the handle. The big fellows are worked from the top or bottom, and a powerful electric motor does the job.

3. Your model is suspended by one thread. The real thing is held up by several strong steel cables.

4. Your model car hangs loose in the elevator shaft. The real car glides in steel tracks that keep it from rattling around.

5. Your model costs 5 cents, the price of the pencil. How much do the big elevators cost?

6. Your model has a 1-mouse carrying capacity. What is the capacity of the real elevator you are examining?

WELLS AND WINDLASSES

Now that you have built an elevator for lifting people (or mice), you should have no trouble in building an elevator for lifting water. There's nothing new in this old-fashioned well and windlass. It is just a piece of this and a bit of that from several projects that have already been described.

You will need 2 milk cartons, a pencil, a hairpin or paper clip, 1 foot of string, and something small and round for a bucket. This can be the top of a ketchup bottle, a very small paper cup, a tiny toy pail, or anything else that looks right for a bucket.

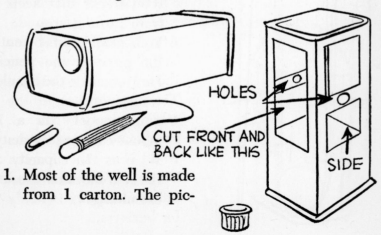

HOLES

CUT FRONT AND BACK LIKE THIS

SIDE

1. Most of the well is made from 1 carton. The pic-

ture shows you how to cut out the openings.

THIS END IS CLOSED

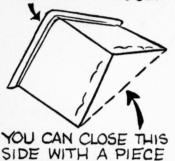

YOU CAN CLOSE THIS SIDE WITH A PIECE OF PAPER

NOTCH

2. The roof of the well is made from a corner of the second carton. If you want an especially pretty job, close up the open side with a three-cornered piece of paper, as shown. Fasten the roof in place with staples or paper fasteners.

3. Cut a notch near one end of the pencil, for fastening the thread when you get to that part of the job. Bend a hairpin or paper clip into a handle shape and push it through the eraser of the pencil. (A needle or compass point will make the hole in the eraser.) Push the pencil through the two holes in the well house.

4. Attach one end of the thread by slipping it into the notch in the pencil.

5. Tie your bucket to the other end of the thread.

6. Pour some water into the well. Now the Eureka Vertical Water Transportation Company is ready for business.

LOADING SKIPS

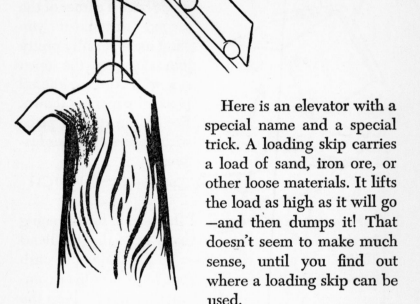

Here is an elevator with a special name and a special trick. A loading skip carries a load of sand, iron ore, or other loose materials. It lifts the load as high as it will go —and then dumps it! That doesn't seem to make much sense, until you find out where a loading skip can be used.

One kind of loading skip is used in steel mills. Its job is to carry a load of iron ore to the top of a blast furnace. Then it dumps the ore into the furnace, to be melted and purified into iron. As you can see, this is no job for human beings. They would be broiled in a minute over the fiery mouth of the furnace. But a loading skip doesn't mind the heat at all.

Another kind of loading skip is used for lifting sand or coal, and then dumping it into a high-up bin called a hopper. Later you will find out how to build a hopper. In the meantime, let's get started on the loading skip.

You will need 2 milk cartons, 2 pencils, 2 thumbtacks, a paper clip, a few feet of thread, and a stapler or some paper fasteners.

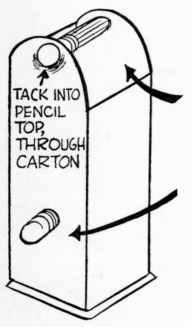

TACK INTO PENCIL TOP, THROUGH CARTON

1. Cut away the top of one carton. Cut as follows: Cut a curve on two opposite sides.

Cut straight pieces out of the remaining sides so that the whole top looks like this.

Make two holes in the sides, large enough for a tight fit of one pencil. Then cut a short piece of the other pencil and fasten it at the top of the carton with tacks.

When you are through, the carton will look like this.

The tower of your loading skip is ready. Now for the bucket, the part that carries the load.

2. Cut a rinsed milk carton across the middle. Then cut away part of 3 sides. Bend the fourth side into the shape shown in the picture.

Punch a small hole in each side, as shown.

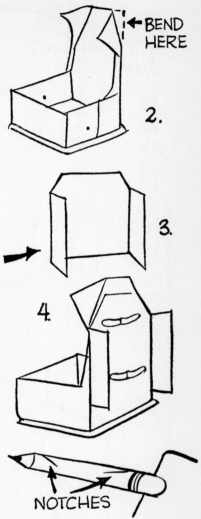

3. The bucket will need a guide to keep it riding straight on its trip up the tower. This guide is a short piece cut in a shape like this.

The piece is then fastened to the back of the bucket. Staples or paper fasteners will do the job.

4. One more step and you're ready to assemble your model. Prepare a pencil-windlass by cutting a notch at each end of a pencil.

Bend a paper clip into a handle shape and push it into the eraser tip.

(It will go in more easily if you first make a hole with the point of your compass.)

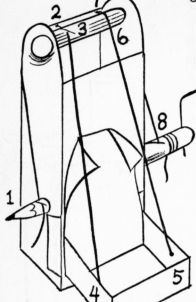

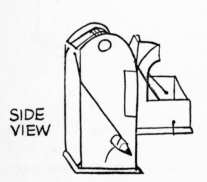

SIDE
VIEW

5. Assembling your model is a simple job. Stick the pencil-windlass in place. Slip one end of a 3-foot piece of thread into one of the notches in the pencil.

Then pass the other end through all the numbered places shown in the picture.

Here is a step-by-step list:

1. Through one notch of the pencil (you have already done this).

2. Through one hole at the top of the tower.

3. Over the short pencil and into the bucket.

4. Through one hole in the bucket.

5. Under the bucket and through the other hole.

6. Up from the bucket and over the short pencil.

7. Through the other hole in the top of the tower.

8. Into the other notch in the pencil.

Now you are all set. Turn the handle and watch the bucket ride up the side of the tower. When it reaches the top, the bucket will tip over to dump its load.

Turn the handle the other way and the bucket rides down to the bottom, ready for another load.

One more piece of advice before you go into business. Don't overload your loading skip. Too heavy a load will cause the sides of the tower to bend inward.

Begin with half a dozen spoonfuls of sand or salt as a test load. Then increase the load a spoonful at a time until you can see that the tower is beginning to complain.

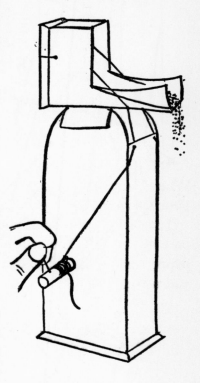

After you have enjoyed your loading skip for a while, you may want to build a hopper for storing the load. You will find directions for building it on the next page.

HOPPERS

A hopper stores sand, coal, or other loose materials. When the hopper is opened at the bottom, the materials pour down into a wheelbarrow, truck, or freight car.

To build your hopper, you will need 1 milk carton and part of another. You will also need a stapler or several paper fasteners, and a short piece of thread, a match, and a paper clip.

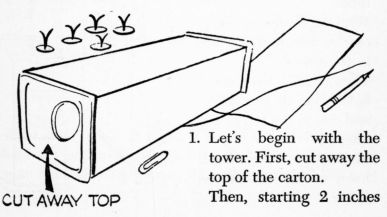

CUT AWAY TOP

1. Let's begin with the tower. First, cut away the top of the carton.
   Then, starting 2 inches

from the top, cut out a piece about 2½ inches long and as wide as the carton.

On the opposite side of the carton, cut out another piece. This piece also starts 2 inches from the top, but it is only about 1½ inches long. This is how the finished tower looks.

2. Now for the chute. This is made of a piece 5 inches long, and as wide as a milk carton. Cut off two corners.

Bend each end into the shape shown in the picture.

With staples or paper fasteners, attach the chute to the tower.

Then make two small holes, one in the chute, and one in the top of the tower.

Make two more small holes in one side of the tower.

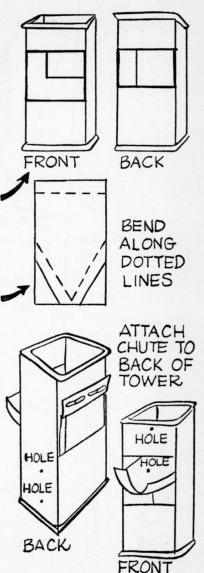

FRONT   BACK

BEND ALONG DOTTED LINES

ATTACH CHUTE TO BACK OF TOWER

HOLE
HOLE
BACK

HOLE
HOLE
FRONT

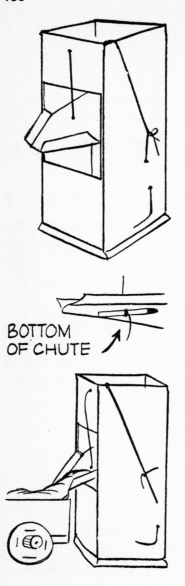

BOTTOM
OF CHUTE

3. Straighten out a paper clip and push it through the two holes in the side of the tower.

Then bend the top end of the clip into a hook shape and the bottom end into an L shape.

Attach a thread to the hook end.

Pass the other end of the thread through the hole in the chute.

Fasten the thread by tying it to a match under the chute.

Now you are ready for work. The paper clip will raise and lower the chute. When the chute is raised, the hopper will store the sand or salt that you dump into it. With the chute lowered, the material will pour down into the dump truck waiting for its load. (Directions for building a dump truck are on pages 85–91.)

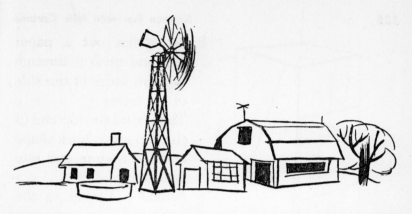

POWER FROM WIND AND WATER

Something for nothing is always a good bargain. The wind costs nothing, yet it can do useful work. It blows sailboats, it turns windmills, it spins the air turbines that pump water or generate electricity on many farms. The wind does these things free of any charge.

You can make a little air turbine in a few minutes. You will need a piece of milk carton, a ruler, a small pencil with an eraser, a compass, a needle, a spool, and half of a snap fastener. The snap fastener should be the solid kind, without a hole in the center.

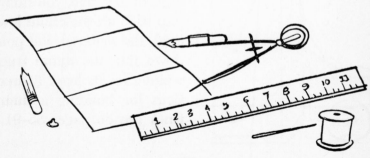

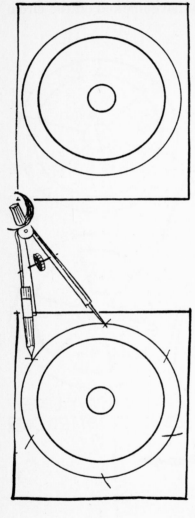

1. Set the points of your compass 1¼ inches apart, and draw a circle on the piece of milk carton. Then set the points 1⅛ inches apart and draw another circle with the same center. Then set the points ¼ inch apart and draw still another circle. The three circles will look like this.

2. Now you need to divide the circle into 6 parts, which is easier than it looks. First set the compass at 1¼ inches, the same size as for the largest circle. Then place the point of the compass anywhere on this largest circle and make a mark with the pencil of the compass, like this.

Now place the point at the pencil mark and make another mark on the circle. Keep placing the point of the compass at each pencil mark, making a new mark each time. As you go around this way you will find that you have marked off the circle into 6 equal parts.

3. Now draw 3 straight lines, joining the 6 marks you have made. Your circle will look like this.

4. With your scissors or knife, cut the heavy lines as shown on this picture. Then bend very carefully along the dotted lines.

5. Cut around the outside circle, leaving a wheel which will be your air turbine. Then make a little hole in the center, just large enough to fit the little bump of the snap fastener. Push the fastener into the hole.

6. Push the needle into the eraser of the pencil and then push the pencil into the spool.

7. Place the air turbine on top of the needle, and you're all set.

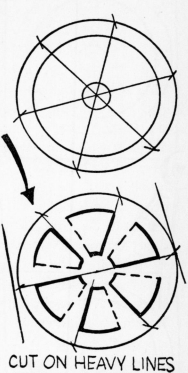

CUT ON HEAVY LINES
BEND ON DOTTED ONES

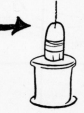

This little air turbine will turn in the slightest breeze. It will show you the direction of the air currents in your room. Hold it over a warm radiator or a lighted lamp, and it will turn one way as the warm rising air pushes up against its blades.

Hold it next to a cold window or beneath the open door of a refrigerator, and it will turn in the opposite direction as the cold, falling air pushes down against it.

Carry it around to various parts of the room and trace the direction of the air currents. You will find that the air currents generally rise over warm places and sink downward over cool places.

Now make a larger air turbine that looks like the kind you sometimes see on farms. For this you will need 2 milk cartons, a compass, a needle, a pencil, an extra eraser and a stapler.

1. Cut the top and bottom from one carton, and then lay the carton flat.

2. Set the compass at 2½ inches. Place the point of the compass on the fold of the carton and draw a circle.

3. Divide the circle into 6 parts, as explained on page 140.

4. With the same center, draw two more circles, with your compass set first at 2¼ inches and then at ½ inch.

5. Draw 3 lines joining the 6 marks on the large circle.

6. Cut the heavy lines shown on this picture. Then bend carefully along the dotted lines.

7. Cut a strip of milk carton paper 6 inches long and ½ inch wide. Make a small needle hole in the center. Then staple the strip to the air turbine, like this.

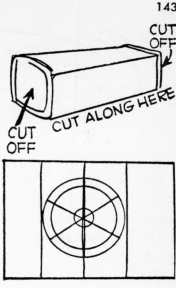

CUT OFF

CUT ALONG HERE

CUT OFF

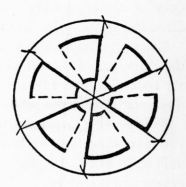

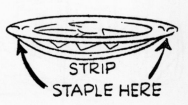

STRIP

STAPLE HERE

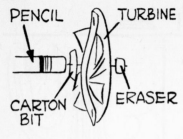

PENCIL   TURBINE

CARTON BIT   ERASER

8. Push the needle into the eraser of the pencil. Then slip on a tiny bit of waxed paper, then your turbine wheel, another piece of waxed paper, and finally a pencil eraser.

Now your turbine wheel is finished, except for its tower. But first test the wheel. Hold the pencil level and blow against the wheel. It should spin briskly, and keep spinning for a few seconds after you stop blowing. If it doesn't, try wiggling the wheel on its needle, to make the holes the tiniest bit larger. Or your wheel may be unbalanced. See if it flops heavily to one position after you spin it. If it does, it is too heavy on one side. A staple or two at the opposite side will help to balance it.

Now let's make the tower. This is fairly easy, taken step by step.

1. Cut away the bottom of a milk carton.
2. Cut a strip out of each side, as in the picture.
3. Take one of these strips and make a "collar" for the top of the tower.
4. Fasten the collar to the tower, using staples or fasteners.
5. Bore a hole at the front

and back of the collar. The easiest way is to start the hole with the point of your compass. Then enlarge it with a sharp-pointed pencil, until it permits a snug fit of the pencil with the wheel attached.

Finished!

Hold your air turbine in a breeze and watch it whirl. Or fasten it to a strip of wood with several thumbtacks and fasten the strip to the side of your window. Then you can lie in bed and say, "It's too windy out today. I think I'll stay in bed and read a book." (This one, for instance.)

Your little air turbine is fun to watch but it can't do any useful work. The real air turbines on farms work either by generating electricity or by pumping water. Here is one hitched to an electric generator.

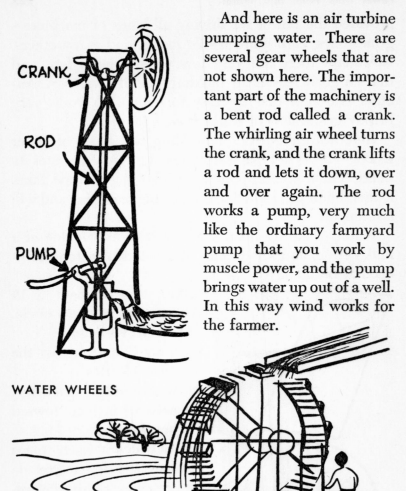

And here is an air turbine pumping water. There are several gear wheels that are not shown here. The important part of the machinery is a bent rod called a crank. The whirling air wheel turns the crank, and the crank lifts a rod and lets it down, over and over again. The rod works a pump, very much like the ordinary farmyard pump that you work by muscle power, and the pump brings water up out of a well. In this way wind works for the farmer.

WATER WHEELS

You have probably seen many pictures of water wheels, but it is very unlikely that you have ever seen a real one, in working condition. At one time water wheels provided the power for driving all kinds of machines—grindstones, corn mills, textile looms, and many others. Nowadays there are very few water wheels left, and that's a good reason for building one of your own. Another reason is that it's easy to build and works very briskly in the flow of water from a faucet.

Here are directions for building two types of water wheel. The first type will take only a few minutes to build, and it works quite well. The second type takes longer, but it looks much more like the real thing and will last longer.

Water wheel Number 1. You will need one side of a milk carton, and a toothpick or a wooden match sharpened at both ends.

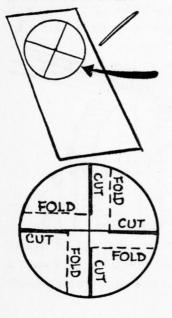

1. Set your compass at 1¼ inches and make a circle. Cut out the circle.
2. Draw 2 lines across the circle, like this.
3. At the end of each line, make a 1-inch cut toward the center.
4. Fold down each piece along the dotted line.
5. With your compass point, make a small hole in the center of the circle.
6. Wiggle your match or toothpick into the hole.

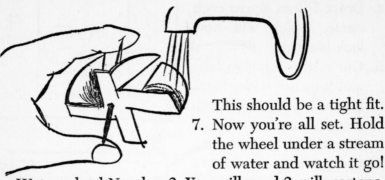

This should be a tight fit.

7. Now you're all set. Hold the wheel under a stream of water and watch it go!

Water wheel Number 2. You will need 2 milk cartons, a compass, a pencil, and a stapler. If you have no stapler you can use paper fasteners, but it will take longer to assemble the wheel.

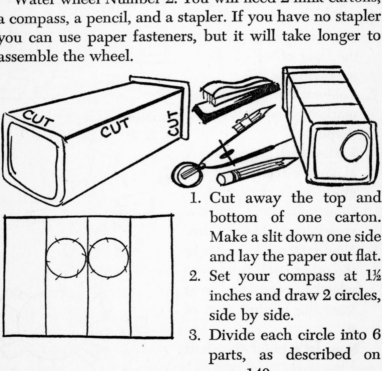

1. Cut away the top and bottom of one carton. Make a slit down one side and lay the paper out flat.

2. Set your compass at 1½ inches and draw 2 circles, side by side.

3. Divide each circle into 6 parts, as described on page 140.

4. Draw 3 lines across each circle, which will now look like this.

5. Cut a strip 6 inches long and 2 inches wide. Mark 2 lines on this strip, each ½ inch from the edge. It should look like this.

6. Cut this strip apart into 6 equal parts. Each part will be 2 inches long and 1 inch wide, and will have the lines of step 5 showing on it, like this.

7. Fold each piece along the marked line, into a U shape.

8. Fasten each piece to one of your circles, with the guide lines of step 4 to show you where. By now your wheel looks like this.

9. Now fasten the pieces to the other circle, and your wheel is complete—or at least the hardest part of it.

Now let's build the shaft and the base.

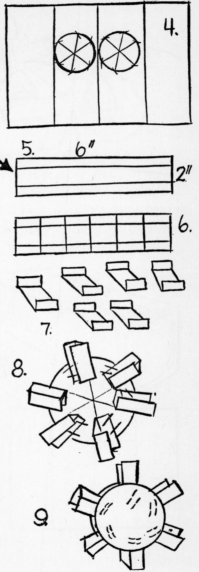

10. The shaft is an ordinary pencil. Prepare 2 holes in the wheel by first pushing in the point of your compass, then widening the holes with a sharp-pointed pencil. This should be a snug fit for the shaft.
11. The base is another milk carton with part of one side cut out, and 2 slots cut into it, like this.

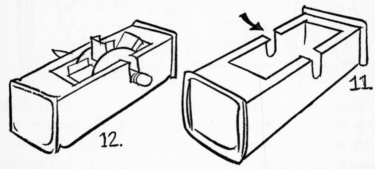

12. Place the shaft in the slots, and you're all set. Hold the wheel in a stream of water from the faucet and watch it whiz.

After you have enjoyed the whizzing for a while (some people can keep this up for hours without getting bored) you may want to try some improvements.

Instead of just having the water wheel whizzing around uselessly, let's put it to work. Let's change the water wheel into a water hoist.

WATER HOIST

Here you see water power at work—very useful work. It is lifting ore from a deep mine up to the surface.

A stream of water, turning a water wheel, causes a rope to be wound around a shaft. At the end of the rope is a bucketful of ore being lifted out of the mine.

Such water hoists were used long ago, before the invention of the steam engine. They were a great improvement over the previous methods of hauling up the ore by hand or by mule power. Water can work without getting tired.

It is very easy to build a water hoist, because most of it is already done. You have already built the water wheel. All you have to add is the hoist.

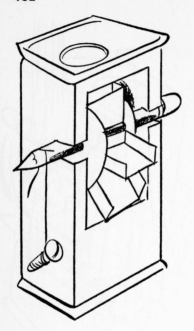

Cut a small notch near one end of the pencil shaft.

Slip one end of a foot-long piece of thread into the notch.

Tie a small weight to the other end of the thread. And that's that.

When you hold the wheel in a stream of water, the wheel will turn and wind up the thread. The thread will lift the weight. Falling water is working for you.

A WATER-WHEEL BELT DRIVE

Here is another way of using the power of falling water. You can hitch up the water wheel so that it drives another machine. For this you will need another pencil, a spool, and a few assorted rubber bands.

1. Push the pencil into the spool.
2. Cut 2 more slots in your milk-carton base, and put the pencil into these slots.
3. Try your various rubber bands for size. Find one that fits snugly, but not tightly, around the spool and the water-wheel shaft.
4. Test your machine under a stream of water. If everything is right, and your rubber band is not too tight or too loose, your water wheel will spin the spool and the pencil on which it is mounted. The spool and pencil represent machinery driven by the wheel.

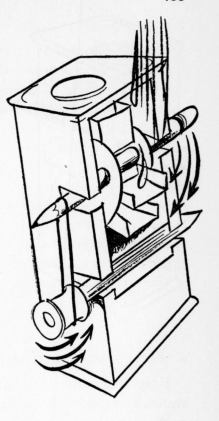

Don't expect perfect results the first time. You will probably have to try several sizes of rubber bands before you find the right one. But when you do the fun will be worth the trouble.

WATER POWER TODAY

You have seen how water power can be used to drive a machine through a belt drive. You have also seen how ore was lifted out of mines by water power. Neither of these methods is used much nowadays.

But water power is used in another way in a great many parts of the world. In fact, you are probably using it right now, if you are reading by electric light. The electricity in your home was made by the rapid turning of an electric generator. Most electric generators are turned by water power. Let's see how.

In this picture you see a special kind of water wheel, called a water turbine. Water from a dam hits the blades of the turbine and causes it to spin.

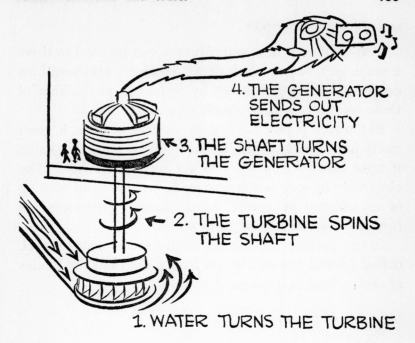

4. THE GENERATOR
   SENDS OUT
   ELECTRICITY

3. THE SHAFT TURNS
   THE GENERATOR

2. THE TURBINE SPINS
   THE SHAFT

1. WATER TURNS THE TURBINE

The spinning turbine causes a long shaft to spin.

This is like the pencil shaft of your homemade water wheel, except that it stands up straight instead of lying down.

At the top of the shaft is an electric generator which is turned by the shaft. The electric generator, when it is turned, sends out electricity to wires that go to your city and to your house.

In this way, you use the power of falling water to light your home, to play your radio, to run your electric trains, and in many other ways.

THE END AND THE BEGINNING

THIS IS the last page of the book, in one way. In another way it's really the beginning, because now you should begin to look around. When you go for a walk, look around for the many kinds of machines that people have invented to make work easier. When you stand among the sidewalk superintendents, watching a building going up, study the pile drivers and derricks and hoisting machines that make light of the heavy work. Find out what makes them go, and how they go, and what they do.

As you watch them at work, you will find that your model-building work has helped you to understand the big machines. In return, looking at the big machines will give you many ideas for new models that you can build. Back and forth, give and take, you'll be the winner both ways.

INDEX

About the Authors

Adrianna Kezar has been associate professor for higher education at the University of Southern California since 2003. She holds a Ph.D. and an M.A. in higher education administration from the University of Michigan. She was formerly editor of the ASHE-ERIC Higher Education Report Series from 1996 to 2004. Kezar has published more than seventy-five journal articles, fifty book chapters, and twelve books. Recent books include: *Recognizing and Serving Low-Income Students in Higher Education* (Routledge Press, 2011) and *Redesigning for Collaboration in Higher Education* (Jossey-Bass, 2009).

Kezar has also served on several editorial boards and received national awards for her commitment and leadership.

Cecile Sam is a doctoral candidate in higher education policy at the Center for Higher Education Policy Analysis at the University of Southern California. Her research interests include leadership and organization theory as applied to faculty work in higher education, with a special interest in ethics.

About the ASHE Higher Education Report Series

Since 1983, the ASHE (formerly ASHE-ERIC) Higher Education Report Series has been providing researchers, scholars, and practitioners with timely and substantive information on the critical issues facing higher education. Each monograph presents a definitive analysis of a higher education problem or issue, based on a thorough synthesis of significant literature and institutional experiences. Topics range from planning to diversity and multiculturalism, to performance indicators, to curricular innovations. The mission of the Series is to link the best of higher education research and practice to inform decision making and policy. The reports connect conventional wisdom with research and are designed to help busy individuals keep up with the higher education literature. Authors are scholars and practitioners in the academic community. Each report includes an executive summary, review of the pertinent literature, descriptions of effective educational practices, and a summary of key issues to keep in mind to improve educational policies and practice.

The Series is one of the most peer reviewed in higher education. A National Advisory Board made up of ASHE members reviews proposals. A National Review Board of ASHE scholars and practitioners reviews completed manuscripts. Six monographs are published each year and they are approximately 120 pages in length. The reports are widely disseminated through Jossey-Bass and John Wiley & Sons, and they are available online to subscribing institutions through Wiley InterScience (http://www.interscience.wiley.com).

Call for Proposals

The ASHE Higher Education Report Series is actively looking for proposals. We encourage you to contact one of the editors, Dr. Kelly Ward (kaward@wsu.edu) or Dr. Lisa Wolf-Wendel (lwolf@ku.edu), with your ideas.

Recent Titles

ORDER FORM SUBSCRIPTION AND SINGLE ISSUES

DISCOUNTED BACK ISSUES:

Use this form to receive 20% off all back issues of *ASHE Higher Education Report*.
All single issues priced at **$23.20** (normally $29.00)

TITLE	ISSUE NO.	ISBN

Call 888-378-2537 or see mailing instructions below. When calling, mention the promotional code JBNND to receive your discount. For a complete list of issues, please visit www.josseybass.com/go/aehe

SUBSCRIPTIONS: (1 YEAR, 6 ISSUES)

☐ New Order ☐ Renewal

U.S.	☐ Individual: $174	☐ Institutional: $265
CANADA/MEXICO	☐ Individual: $174	☐ Institutional: $325
ALL OTHERS	☐ Individual: $210	☐ Institutional: $376

*Call 888-378-2537 or see mailing and pricing instructions below.
Online subscriptions are available at www.onlinelibrary.wiley.com*

ORDER TOTALS:

Issue / Subscription Amount: $ _____

Shipping Amount: $ _____
(for single issues only – subscription prices include shipping)

Total Amount: $ _____

SHIPPING CHARGES:
First Item $5.00
Each Add'l Item $3.00

(No sales tax for U.S. subscriptions. Canadian residents, add GST for subscription orders. Individual rate subscriptions must be paid by personal check or credit card. Individual rate subscriptions may not be resold as library copies.)

BILLING & SHIPPING INFORMATION:

☐ **PAYMENT ENCLOSED:** *(U.S. check or money order only. All payments must be in U.S. dollars.)*

☐ **CREDIT CARD:** ☐ VISA ☐ MC ☐ AMEX

Card number _____ Exp. Date _____

Card Holder Name _____ Card Issue # _____

Signature _____ Day Phone _____

☐ **BILL ME:** *(U.S. institutional orders only. Purchase order required.)*

Purchase order # _____
Federal Tax ID 13559302 • GST 89102-8052

Name _____

Address _____

Phone _____ E-mail _____

Copy or detach page and send to: **John Wiley & Sons, PTSC, 5th Floor**
989 Market Street, San Francisco, CA 94103-1741

Order Form can also be faxed to: **888-481-2665**

PROMO JBNND